D0596959

DEAD TREE PRESS

Library of Congress Cataloging-In-Publication Data

Jacobs, Scott, 1950-
Donald Trump: The Awful Years / Stump Connolly

ISBN: 978-1-879652-29-3 (hardcover)
ISBN: 978-1-879652-20-0 (paperback)
ISBN: 978-1-879652-22-4 (ebook)

Includes index

1. Politics. 2. Media. 3. United States–History I. Title

First Edition 2021
Printed in the United States

I Told You So!

by Stump Connolly

Dead Tree Press

Also by Stump Connolly

STUMP, A Campaign Journal
Talk's Cheap, Let's Race
The Long Slog

documentary
Road to The Presidency: Inside the Clinton Campaign

*"Don't give him credit for the vaccines.
The vaccines were me."*

–Donald Trump
November 27, 2020

Contents

Prologue

    1   Statesman of the Year (2012)

Republican Convention

    7   The Republicans: Day One

    9   "Lock Her Up!"

    15   Mike Pence on Fire

    19   Our Mussolini

Democratic Convention

    27   A Heavy Lift

    31   A Punch in the Mouth! (Joe Biden)

    35   The Has-Been

    39   One Man's Opinion

2016 Election

    47   Can We Talk?

    53   Hate vs. Fear

Down the Rabbit Hole

    63   Down the Rabbit Hole

    69   Impeachment—How and When

    75   All in on The Wall

    79   The Salesman in Chief

    85   The Environment Is Overrated

    95   Trump's First 100 Days

    101   The National Conversation

    109   I Am a Rock, I Am an Island, I Am an Idiot

    115   Not the Only Show in Town

    119   The Lonely Life of I Alone

    125   Watch Out for That Flying Bag of Dope

Russia

    131   Trump Did It!

    137   The Russian Connection

    143   In the Room Where it Happened (John Bolton)

Live by the Tweet, Die by the Tweet

    155   Stump's Twitter Feed

Shipwreck

    175   Keeping Score

    177   To Mask or Not to Mask

    181   The Press Conference

    185   Shoe on the Other Foot

The End Is Near

    191   Never in Doubt

    201   See You in Court

    207   The Big Kahuna of Lies

    215   Loser

    219   Biden Masks

    225   Tis the Season to Be Bad

    231   An Avalanche of Chaos, Corruption and Confusion

You Mean It's Not Over

    241   A Constitutional Crisis, Trump Style

    249   Impeachment, Again

    255   Unity

    259   The Last Hurrah

    263   The Mob Was Fed Lies

Epilogue

    273   The Note in the Desk

Photo Credits   274

Index   276

Prologue

Statesman of the Year

A HURRICANE DESCENDED ON SOUTH FLORIDA Sunday night for the start of the Republican convention. Not Hurricane Isaac, but Donald Trump taking time out from his busy schedule to accept the Statesman of the Year Award from the Sarasota County Republican Party.

Storm winds pummeled the two bridges I had to cross to get to the ceremony, but all was sunny in Sarasota. I pulled into the driveway of the Ritz-Carlton Hotel past a procession of limos waiting for the valet. No TV trucks were in sight. It was just me and a thousand of the richest people in Florida.

Sarasota is a bastion of wealth, and much of it is old wealth. The scions of families who made their fortunes in lumber, insurance and real estate flock to Sarasota to manage their foundations, so everyone in the room seemed to know everyone else. Men in tailored suits and women in designer gowns mingled in the lobby. "These people don't have a million dollars, they have tens of millions," a financial adviser told me. They thought nothing of paying $150 to hear Trump, or $1,000 more to get their picture taken with him. He was certainly a step up from Haley Barbour, last year's honoree.

When the lights dimmed, the sound system blared "Money, Money, Money," and Trump sauntered out on stage. He pointed to people in the audience he knew and grinned broadly at those he didn't. Everyone stood and applauded. A woman at my table lifted two fingers to her lips to whistle and swung her jewel-encrusted purse around like a lariat.

Trump was introduced by Joe Gruters, the Sarasota Republican chairman, as "Tornado Trump"—a man who has had a whirlwind career. From humble origins in Queens, Joe told how he became a real estate mogul in New York, a TV star, owner of golf courses, hotels, casinos all over the world—"Come on, Joe," Trump shouted. "These people want to get out of here." And they did. They roared their approval. Then Trump stepped to the podium, no notes, no teleprompter, no clear idea what he was going to say, and he spoke. He opened with an apocalyptic vision of America.

"We are in a country that is in decline. Now we can say oh, that's not so. And we can say, no we're not, we're doing great. But we're not doing great. Even here, I see so many different signs on houses...for sale...for sale...for sale...owner-financed housing available, you know, because the banks aren't lending."

And it was all Obama's fault. He bailed out the banks but didn't demand more lending. He let unemployment rise to 8.3%. "But really when you look behind the definitions, it's 21," he said. "We have a country that has serious, serious trouble. If we have four more years of President Barack Obama, we're not going to have a country left."

"We have somebody in office that truly doesn't have a clue. He never built anything. He never made a deal except to buy his house, and if you want to look into that deal, there was a lot of monkey business going on, I can tell you. He doesn't know how things work."

But Obama didn't ruin America alone. China helped. China, China, China. They were manipulating their currency, stealing our jobs and outwitting us at every turn. Obama was soft on China when he should have been beating their ass. That's why Trump was backing Mitt Romney. Romney was a businessman.

Then Trump offered his definition of a good businessman.

"I've always heard if you were a successful businessman you can't run for office. I see so many successful people who want to run, but during the course of their success, they beat the hell out of people. They won. There's no shame in that. They've been tough. They've been competitive. They worked. They built their business, and honestly, they made enemies.

"So now they want to run a state, a country, or something, and they can't win...They can't put it together. They can't really go out there because all of those people that they beat consistently over a lifetime...all of those people come back to haunt you.

"And I see it happening with Mitt. Mitt was a successful man. He did a great job. Look at Staples. You do a hundred great deals, and you do one that didn't work out. All they want to talk about is the one that didn't work out. It's terrible."

But Trump wasn't finished. How about the Obama people? Those people were vicious. They'd stop at nothing. Did you see what they did to Hillary?

"So you have to fight fire with fire," he said. "You've got to not be so politically correct. We are in the fight of our lives, and it's like I told Mitt and Paul, you've got to get nasty."

— August 27, 2012

*Republican
Convention*

The Republicans:
Day One

THE REPUBLICAN CONVENTION KICKED OFF in Cleveland Monday with Paul Manafort, Donald Trump's campaign manager, calling John Kasich, the governor of Ohio, an embarrassment for not attending a convention in his own state, and Kasich saying it will be a cold day in hell before he does.

Protestors gathered outside, and the opening moments featured a floor fight over whether to accept Trump's agenda for the proceedings. A loud chorus of No's went up on the floor. The chair ruled the ayes have it. The Colorado delegation walked out.

If you were looking for excitement, how about opening remarks from Scott Baio, a now grown-up bit character on *Happy Days*. How did he get the nod? Simple. He was in the green room at Fox last week, and Trump asked him to do it. "Guys like me don't get to do this kind of stuff often," he told CNN.

Or Antonio Sabato Jr., the Calvin Klein underwear model who followed him. "Barack Obama and Hillary Clinton promote division," he said. "Don't be fooled. Donald Trump is for unity." Or Gen. Michael Flynn, recently fired by Obama as head of the Defense Intelligence Agency and now national security adviser to Trump. He went on about the way Clinton had failed to safeguard America and concluded she ought to be thrown in jail for sending out State Department emails on her private account.

"Lock her up!" the crowd responded.

Next up was the evening's main event. The lights went dark, and the nominee himself appeared in silhouette at the back of the stage, a white glow rising from the floor to illuminate his face. The first words out of his mouth were: "We're going to win. We're going to win so big." Then he introduced his wife.

Melania Trump gave one of the best speeches of the night, a heartfelt tribute to the values her parents taught her growing up in Slovenia. Only they weren't her values, they were Michelle Obama's, plagiarized from her address to the 2008 Democratic convention.

But wait. There's more. An hour more of lesser Republican candidates getting their time in the spotlight. "This is Convention 101. You put your highlight at the end," David Brooks said shaking his head. But no one was there to hear him. Two-thirds of the delegates had left.

We're off to a great start.

— July 18, 2016

'Lock Her Up!'

"SO FAR, SO GOOD," SARAH PALIN TWEETED Tuesday morning from Alaska. "From 3,000 miles up North, it's good to hear the GOP Convention is going well."

It was a day for hunting down plagiarists. Melania's speech sparked the first real controversy of the convention. "It was only 70 words in three passages," Sean Spicer told MSNBC, no worse than lifting a few inspirational phrases from *My Little Pony*. "After all this is over, I think people are going to say this was a great convention. The stage looked phenomenal."

"What this shows is that the Trump campaign is little more than an advance staff and a Twitter feed," said Dan Senor, a Republican strategist close to Mike Pence.

No Negs Here

But enough with the negativity. No one has been shot yet. Eleven staff members of the California delegation did contract a virus and were sent to a motel outside Cleveland to quarantine. The good news is the virus only lasts three days. The bad news is it causes vomiting and diarrhea. So if you see any Republicans vomiting or shitting on each other, please report them to the authorities.

The roll call to make Donald J. Trump the official presidential nominee of the Republican Party didn't take long. The final tally was:

- Donald Trump, 1,725
- Ted Cruz, 475
- John Kasich, 120
- Marco Rubio, 114
- Ben Carson, 7
- Jeb Bush, 3
- Rand Paul, 2
- [1,237 delegates needed to win.]

Trump's victory was sealed when his son Donald Jr. led the New York delegation in casting 87 votes for his father. "Who says the crowd is going wild?" *Politico*'s Roger Simon tweeted. "The only thing going wild are the graphics on the big screen."

Make America Work

The theme of the night was "Make America Work Again"—a goal that apparently can only be accomplished by sending Hillary Clinton to jail.

Speaking on behalf of work were:

- Dana White, president of the Ultimate Fighting Championship (UFC), who staged his mixed martial arts bouts in Trump casinos when no one else would have them.
- Asa Hutchinson, the first-term governor of Arkansas who bragged that unemployment in his state was the lowest it has been in history, no thanks to President Obama.

- Andy Wist, head of Standard Waterproofing, a Bronx roofing company who believes "working men and women still matter in this country."
- And Natalie Gulbis, a professional golfer on the LPGA tour who appeared in a recent *Sports Illustrated* swimsuit issue wearing only body paint. Sorry, none of the cable channels covered her remarks so I don't know what she had to add.

The TV networks joined the party two hours later, and a couple politicians took a crack at it: Paul Ryan, the party's vice presidential candidate only four years earlier, and Senate Majority Leader Mitch McConnell. Ryan gave one of those "Win One for the Gipper" speeches calling on all Republicans to rally to the cause. McConnell was lukewarm in his praise of Trump, mentioning him only six times, but taking 26 potshots at Clinton. If there was any drama to be had, it came from New Jersey Gov. Chris Christie promising to prosecute Hillary for her crimes against America.

Too Much Fun

"Let's do something fun," Christie said. "As a former prosecutor, I welcome this opportunity to hold Hillary Clinton accountable for her performance and her character."

He then proceeded to present the case "on facts." He ticked off Clinton's alleged misdeeds in Libya, Nigeria, China, Syria, Iran, Russia, and, of course, in her personal emails, egging the crowd on after each count of the indictment to shout "Guilty!"

But they were having none of it. They had so much fun with Gen. Flynn chanting "Lock her up!" they shouted it even louder so it is now emerging as the convention's main theme.

"What happened to jobs and the economy night?" an incredulous Gloria Borger asked a panel of CNN commentators. "I felt like I was at the Salem Witch Trials," chimed in Michael Smerconish. Over on CBS, Bob Schieffer, attending his 24th presidential convention, said this was turning into "a doom and gloom convention."

A Son's Tribute

Donald Trump Jr. brought the delegates back on track with a tribute to the hardest working man in America, his dad.

"You want to know what kind of president he'll be? Let me tell you how he ran his businesses, and I know because I was there with him by his side on job sites and in conference rooms from the time I could walk. He didn't hide out behind some desk in an executive suite, he spent his career with regular Americans. He hung out with the guys on construction sites pouring concrete and hanging sheetrock. He listened to them and he valued their opinions as much and often more than the guys from Harvard and Wharton locked away in offices away from the real work.

"He promoted people based on their character, their street smarts and their work ethic, not simply paper credentials," he went on. "His true gift as a leader is that he sees the potential in people that other executives would overlook because their resumes don't include the names of fancy colleges and degrees."

Junior's speech lasted 12 minutes. Unfortunately, there were 48 more minutes to go.

Clint Eastwood Without the Chair

It was time for Ben Carson to do his thing. At one point, Carson led the Republican primary field. He is one of only 80 Black delegates at the convention (out of 2,473) and he was his usual poised, confident self, spouting his usual gibberish. One of the problems with Hillary Clinton, he said, was that she wrote her senior thesis at Wellesley about Chicago-based community organizer Saul Alinsky.

Alinsky's manifesto *Rules for Radicals*, Carson said, offers an "over-the-shoulder acknowledgment of the very first radical who rebelled against the establishment and did it so effectively that he at least won his own kingdom." And what was his name? Lucifer. In Carson's mind, this made Hillary the disciple of a devil worshipper, and thus, worthy of being locked up.

"Ben Carson is Clint Eastwood without the chair," Democratic strategist Ben LaBolt sniffed afterward.

How Did It Play?

With 30 minutes still to go, and more than half the chairs on the convention floor empty, a CNN roundtable tried to wrap up. David Axelrod, the political strategist who organized two Obama conventions, was dumbfounded. Why would the Republicans waste so much precious primetime on this? "When you have a Donald Trump Jr., why do you follow him with Carson and Kimberlin Brown?" Brown is a former soap opera star on *The Young and the Restless* and now an avocado grower/interior decorator in California.

"We asked the campaign about that," Anderson Cooper replied, "and they say this is the way Mr. Trump wants it. It's his convention, and this is what he wants."

Republican Sen. Ben Sasse said earlier in the week he'd rather watch dumpster fires in Nebraska than attend this convention. Can't wait to see what Sarah Palin thinks.

— July 19, 2016

Mike Pence
on Fire

WHAT COULD BE MORE EXCITING than a vice presidential acceptance speech by Mike Pence? And how are those dumpster fires looking out there in Nebraska, Senator Sasse?

Wednesday was the day the Republican Convention was supposed to pivot, another popular word in politics this year signifying a turn from hurling brickbats at Hillary to throwing laurels on their own candidate, Donald Trump.

The lingering effects of Melania's plagiarism were dispensed with early in the day when the Trump Organization issued a statement acknowledging

Melania cribbed whole sections of her speech on Trump family values from Michelle Obama. Never mind that a few hours earlier Paul Manafort was telling reporters the allegations were absurd.

The mastermind, the wizard himself, tweeted out: "Good news is Melania's speech got more publicity than any in the history of politics especially if you believe that all press is good press." And with that, the scandal was swept into the dustbin like so many shards of broken glass.

Losers Night

Wednesday was Losers Night, a chance for some of Trump's vanquished primary opponents—Scott Walker, Newt Gingrich, Marco Rubio and Ted Cruz—to step to the podium to kiss the ring of the party's anointed choice. Yet another Trump progeny, Eric, would extol his father; and Pence, the Indiana governor known for nothing, would wrap it all up with a call for unity.

That's the way it was supposed to go. But Florida Gov. Rick Scott never got the message. He opened the ceremony with a tribute to the Orlando nightclub victims that quickly became a call to war against radical Islamic terrorism. "The war is real. It is here in America," he said. "And the next president must destroy that evil. Donald Trump is that man."

"Lock her up!" the delegates shouted.

The Mystery of Ted Cruz

Ted Cruz's speech was the most anticipated. During the primaries, Trump had insulted his wife, planted false stories about extramarital affairs in the *National Enquirer*, linked his father to a plot to assassinate JFK, and freely bandied about his favorite epithet, Lyin' Ted Cruz.

The Texas senator, in turn, called Trump "a sniveling coward," "a pathological liar," "utterly amoral," "a serial philanderer," and "a narcissist at a level that I don't think this country has ever seen."

With more delegates in the hall than any other second-place finisher, Cruz acted like he was giving his own acceptance speech. He spoke slowly, extending his 12-minute time slot to 23. He talked about freedom. He's for it. And slavery. He's against it. All the while building a crescendo to what Trump forces hoped would be The Endorsement.

"We deserve leaders who stand for principle. Unite us all behind shared values. Cast aside anger for love. That is the standard we should expect, from everybody," Cruz said. The crowd waited for the next sentence with bated breath. The words they wanted to hear did not come. "And to those listening, please, don't stay home in November."

Suddenly, the mood turned ugly. Trump glowered at Cruz from the back of the hall, stealing focus from the podium. The digital screen behind Cruz started to mysteriously flicker.

"And vote your conscience, vote for candidates up and down the ticket who you trust to defend our freedom and to be faithful to the Constitution," Cruz continued.

The New York delegation seated in front began to boo. Many held out their arms with thumbs down. "I appreciate the enthusiasm of the New York delegation," Cruz snapped.

But the damage was done. Catcalls rained in from all parts of the hall. Trump walked stone-faced to the family VIP section. The flickering stage screen—the one that party spokesman Sean Spicer had called phenomenal only the day before—went dead.

The Twittersphere was exploding with vitriol, all aimed at Cruz. Chris Christie called him a disgrace. Mike Huckabee said he should never be allowed to hold office again. The Virginia attorney general had to escort Cruz's wife Heidi out of the hall to protect her from irate delegates.

Oh yeah, and Mike Pence spoke.

A Christian, a Conservative and a Republican

"I'm a Christian, a conservative and a Republican, in that order," Pence began, "and honestly, I never thought I'd be standing here." Neither did anyone else.

In the dulcet tones of a choirboy, looking like a polished political nesting doll, Pence explained why he is the perfect balance to Trump on the ticket.

"I grew up on the front row of the American dream," Pence said. "I was raised in a small town in southern Indiana, in a big family with a cornfield in the backyard. And if you know anything about Hoosiers, you know we love to suit up and compete…. We play to win. That's why I joined this campaign in a heartbeat. You have nominated a man who never quits, who never backs down, a fighter, a winner."

Pence said he spoke for all the people who are "tired of being told a little intellectual elite in a far distant capital can plan our lives for us better than we can plan them ourselves."

"You know, Donald Trump gets it. He's the genuine article. He's a doer in a game usually reserved for talkers. And when Donald Trump does his talking, he doesn't tiptoe around the rules of political correctness. He's his own man. Distinctly American. And where else would a man like him find a following than in the land of the free and the home of the brave."

Pence tested out a few of the attack lines he's supposed to use against Hillary Clinton. She's "America's Secretary of the Status Quo." She "personifies the establishment in Washington."

"I guarantee you, when Donald Trump becomes president the change will be huge," he said. "And the funny thing is the party in power seems helpless to figure out our nominee. The media has the same problem. They keep thinking they've done him in, and they wake up finding the man is still standing and running stronger than ever before. The man just doesn't quit."

The Aftermath

The pundits were punishing in the aftermath. There is always an aftermath in cable news. "This convention is a mess," Chuck Todd said. "You have now messed up the Mike Pence rollout twice. Unbelievable!"

Before he signed off, Brian Williams held up the front pages of the next day's *Boston Herald* and New York *Daily News*. Pence's speech was nowhere to be found.

"BOOS CRUZ" blared the *Herald*.

"CIVIL WAR!" crowed the *Daily News*.

"And there you have it. Night Three of the Republican Convention," Williams sighed.

— July 21, 2016

Our Mussolini

THERE IS NO FAIR AND BALANCED WAY TO SAY THIS. The acceptance speech Donald Trump gave at the Republican Convention Thursday night was the most frightening piece of demagoguery I've ever heard in politics.

Over the course of his 75-minute oration—one pundit called it Castro-sized—Trump gave America a taste of the bravado that has mesmerized Republicans for months. Sure, he stuck to his prepared remarks, but the performance had the same incendiary rhetoric, conflated facts and dog whistles that ignited his campaign. He opened by promising to present the facts plainly and honestly and share with you his plan of action for America.

"We cannot afford to be so politically correct anymore," he said, drawing the first of many standing ovations. But it was soon clear his plan of action for America boiled down to one thing.

Elect Me!

Let me give you just a short list of his plan. "I will add millions of new jobs and trillions in new wealth that can be used to rebuild America... restore law and order...put Republicans on the Supreme Court...appoint the best prosecutors and law enforcement officials...build a great border wall to stop illegal immigration... stop drugs from pouring into our country...be considerate and compassionate to everyone...turn our bad trade agreements into great ones...build the roads, highways, bridges, tunnels, airports, and the railways of tomorrow...rescue kids from failing schools... repeal and replace Obamacare...and fix TSA at the airports."

Malarkey

And how is Trump going to do that?

"I have proposed the largest tax reduction of any candidate."

Promises, promises. What you have proposed is a corporate tax reduction, light on tax relief for the middle class, that will add a trillion dollars a year to our national debt. That's the same national debt you said you are going to cut.

"We will rescue kids from failing schools."

That might be hard given that you've pledged to eliminate the Department of Education.

"I will ask myself: Does this make life better for young Americans in Baltimore, Chicago, Detroit, Ferguson?"

How about going there to ask them?

"I am going to work very hard to protect free speech for all Americans."

This from a man who taunts reporters at his rallies and wants to loosen up the libel laws so he can sue people who criticize him.

*"I have made billions of dollars in business making deals—now
I'm going to make our country rich again."*

Says the man who went bankrupt four times. Maybe what he means
is that he's run every scam imaginable on the tax system, and he's happy
to share his insight into loopholes, tax dodges, write-offs, and offsetting
depreciation.

*"Nobody knows that system better than me, which is why I alone
can fix it."*

But he alone cannot fix it. Say what you will about Hillary Clinton,
she knows our government is made up of three branches: the legislative,
the executive and the judiciary. There are 300,000 people in the federal
workforce in Washington alone, and they all operate in their own little
fiefdoms. Hillary has spent a lifetime in the White House, Senate and State
Department trying to get this behemoth of a government to work together.

Donald Trump seems to think it's all run by a switch in the Oval
Office. In Trump's world, he runs the show. He makes the deals. He dictates which projects he will pursue. If you believe his kids, he's down there
in the trenches pouring the concrete for his high rises. But what he does
best is sell himself.

There's no *there* there in Trump's bluster. But one thing is sure, all we
need to do to cure America's problems is let him make all the decisions.

"I alone can fix it."

Speaking of Hillary

And speaking of Hillary, did Trump mention her?

Do wild bears shit in the woods?

"Hillary Clinton is proposing mass amnesty, mass immigration, and
mass lawlessness," he said. Her immigration ideas are "radical and dangerous." She has committed "terrible, terrible crimes" by using her private
server to send emails while she was secretary of state. "Her single greatest
accomplishment may be committing such an egregious crime and getting
away with it—especially when others have paid so dearly."

"Lock her up!" the crowd chanted.

"Her bad instincts and bad judgment" underlie the crisis in the Middle East. "Iran is on the path to nuclear weapons. Syria is engulfed in a civil war and a refugee crisis that threatens the world. After 15 years of wars in the Middle East, after trillions of dollars spent and thousands of lives lost, the situation is worse than it ever has been before. This is the legacy of Hillary Clinton. Death, Destruction, Terrorism and Weakness."

Those, of course, are not Hillary's only sins, Trump noted in passing. She also wants to protect bureaucrats, take jobs away from steelworkers and abolish the Second Amendment. But you get the idea. She's a bad person. You might call her "crooked."

But I'll tell you one thing. I'll take a woman whose worst crime is using an iPhone over a demagogue with his finger on the nuclear button. What does it profit a party to gain the Supreme Court and lose the world in a megalomaniac's nuclear war?

— July 22, 2016

Democratic
Convention

A Heavy Lift

IF YOU FOLLOW POLITICS, you'll notice there are certain watchwords that tie together the media coverage. When all 17 of the Republican contenders were bunched at the starting line in Iowa, everyone was talking about what lane they were running in. When Donald Trump emerged from the field, the talk turned to how he would pivot at the Republican convention.

On Monday, the Democratic Convention opened in Philadelphia, and all the reporters could talk about was the "heavy lift" Hillary Clinton will have. As Trump's dark and desultory acceptance speech demonstrated, her first job at this convention is to lift the spirits of America.

News commentators like to measure the mood of the nation in right track/wrong track numbers. The latest polls show 69% of Americans think we are on the wrong track. But that figure is misleading.

In the 45 years since George Gallop first asked the question, Americans have almost never believed the country was on the right track. Today's number is right around where it usually is. It could be worse. In 2008, on the verge of Obama's first election, 91% of Americans thought we were on the wrong track.

When Donald Trump announced his candidacy a year ago, 62% of Americans thought our country was on the wrong track. The seven-point rise is nothing special, especially if you consider four of those points have come in the last 20 days after shootings in Orlando, Dallas, Baton Rouge and Nice.

Happiness is Illusive

Happiness is hard to measure. But it was readily apparent Saturday when Hillary Clinton introduced her running mate Virginia Sen. Tim Kaine in Miami. The rollout was everything Trump's introduction of Mike Pence was not. Joyful, upbeat, and packed to the rafters with all the colors of America's rainbow population. Hillary never looked better, and the guy behind her with the happy-as-a-clam smile on his face looked okay too.

Her introduction took 17 minutes. (Trump talked 28 minutes before even mentioning his running mate, old What's His Name.) While Hillary sat on a stool paying rapt attention, Kaine regaled the crowd with anecdotes about his improbable rise from son of an ironworker to the nomination for the second highest office in the land.

He spoke about his victories as a civil rights lawyer. He slipped fluently back and forth between English and Spanish, a language he learned as a missionary in Honduras. He boasted of his winning record in past elections and his greatest victory, marrying Anne Holton, now the Virginia secretary of education.

James Fallows, national correspondent for *The Atlantic*, said it was the most impressive introduction of a politician he'd ever seen. Andrea Mitchell called it "a home run." After Kaine spoke, he could have taken three laps around the bases before the roar of the crowd died down.

WikiLeaks

But the euphoria was short-lived. While Clinton and Kaine were parading around the stage, WikiLeaks was releasing 20,000 private emails hacked off the Democratic National Committee server. They showed party officials taking potshots at Bernie Sanders and, in effect, trying to tip the scales for Hillary during the primaries.

The controversy ricocheted around the Sunday morning talk shows. On CNN, Sanders pooh-poohed the revelation as nothing he didn't already know. Jake Tapper baited him with a question. Did he agree with Hillary's choice of Kaine over Sen. Elizabeth Warren? "Look, we're Democrats," he answered. "We disagree. But even on his worst, worst, worst day, Tim Kaine is a thousand times better than Donald Trump."

It's All Show Business

By Sunday night, DNC Chairwoman Debbie Wasserman Schultz was gone, but Sanders supporters were not easily mollified. As they demonstrated outside, the Democrats rolled out a cavalcade of stars to get their convention underway. Eva Longoria, Demi Lovato, comedians Al Franken and Sarah Silverman, one a Clinton delegate and the other a Sanders supporter, introducing Paul Simon to sing "Bridge Over Troubled Water."

New Jersey Sen. Cory Booker invoked Maya Angelou's poem "Still I Rise" in his keynote.

> *You may write me down in history*
> *With your bitter, twisted lies,*
> *You may trod me in the very dirt*
> *But still, like dust, I'll rise.*

Booker spoke of an America that could turn the corner from despair to aspiration, but only if all its parts were working in unison. "This is our history: escaped slaves, knowing that liberty is not secure for some until it's secure for all, sometimes hungry, often hunted, in dark woods and deep swamps, they looked up to the North Star and said with a determined whisper, America, we will rise."

Speaker after speaker rose to explain why "I'm with Hillary." Some spoke of Hillary passion for child welfare, disabilities, women's rights. All of them were just preamble for the night's feature attraction, first lady Michelle Obama leveraging all of her popularity to bend the arc of public favor toward Hillary.

I'm With Hillary

To get to the headline, Michelle slayed. She talked about her family values—the same family values that inspired Melania Trump to plagiarize her—and how they helped her get through a White House stint that began watching her daughters go off for their first day of school in two black SUVs surrounded by men with guns, and ended with her oldest, Malia, graduating from high school.

She spoke of the importance parents play as role models. "With every word we utter, with every action we take, we know our kids are watching us," she said, and that responsibility carries over into politics "because we know that our words and our actions matter, not just to our girls, but the children across this country."

This opened the door for her to praise Hillary's "lifelong devotion to our nation's children" and, not subtly, Trump's lack of it. "I want someone who knows this job and takes it seriously. Someone who understands that the issues the president faces are not black and white and cannot be boiled down to 140 characters." This election isn't about which candidate is better or worse, she concluded. "It's about one thing and one thing only. It's about leaving something better for our kids."

"I'm with Hillary" may be one of the lamest political slogans in modern politics. Hillary doesn't have Trump's charisma, and she's not an inspiring speaker. She's a hard worker who cares about the right things. Just who you want on the team for a heavy lift. She's not running for president as America's savior, she's running as the party standard-bearer. Her strength is the army of people behind her. They're the ones who will vote in this election. She's just carrying the flag.

— July 26, 2016

A Punch in
the Mouth!

ANYBODY WHO WAITED FOR ABC, CBS and NBC to break into their primetime entertainment for the third night of the Democratic convention missed it.

Sure, you got to see Tim Kaine give his first speech as a vice presidential nominee and Barack Obama give one of his last as President. But they were both the kind of political orations you watch with graham crackers and a glass of warm milk on the coffee table.

If you're the kind of guy who likes to talk politics over a beer and bucket of hot wings at Hooters, you should have tuned in an hour earlier for Joe Biden's takedown of Donald Trump.

Biden took the stage to the strains of "Rocky"—a not-so-subtle nod to his role as the Democrats' attack dog. He was in a valedictory mood when he began, thanking his wife and family, noting the absence of his son Beau who died of cancer last year, and paying homage to Barack and Michelle for the eight greatest years of his life.

He offered the requisite tribute to Hillary Clinton as smart, tough and passionate. "If you live in a neighborhood like the one I grew up in, you worry about your job and getting decent pay. If you worry about your children's education, if you are taking care of an elderly parent, then there is only one person in this election who will help you, only one person in this race who will be there, who has always been there for you," he said. "That's not just who she is, it is her life story."

Then he got down to what he really came here to say:

"Ladies and gentlemen, to state the obvious, I'm not trying to be a wise guy here, I really mean it. That's not Donald Trump's story."

The hall erupted. "Just listen to me a second without booing or cheering," he chastised them. And the hall fell silent.

"His cynicism is unbounded. His lack of empathy and compassion can be summed up in that phrase I suspect he is most proud of making famous: 'You're fired.' I mean, really, I'm not joking. Think about that. Think about everything you learned as a child. No matter where you were raised, how can there be pleasure in saying, 'You're fired'?"

There are speeches woven together with words, and speeches composed in the pauses. This was a speech of pauses. So I'm going to give you the rest with only a few omissions and none of those pesky quotation marks.

He is trying to tell us he cares about the middle class.

Give me a break.

That is a bunch of malarkey!

Whatever he thinks, and I mean this from the bottom of my heart—I know I'm called middle-class Joe and in Washington, that is not meant as a compliment. It means you are not sophisticated—I know why we are strong. I know why we are held together. It's because there has always been a growing middle class.

This guy does not have a clue about the middle class.

Not a clue.

Because folks, when the middle class does well, the rich do very well and the poor have hope. They have a way out. He has no clue about what makes America great.

Actually, he has no clue.

Period.

Folks, let me say something that has nothing to do with politics. Let me talk about something that I'm deadly serious about.

This is a complicated and uncertain world we live in. The threats are too great, the times are too uncertain, to elect Donald Trump as president of the United States. No major party, no major party nominee in the history of the nation has ever known less or been less prepared to deal with our national security.

We cannot elect a man who exploits our fears of ISIS…who embraces the tactics of our enemies. We cannot elect a man who belittles our closest allies while embracing dictators like Vladimir Putin.

I mean it.

A man who seeks to sow division in America for his own gain and creates disorder around the world. A man who confuses bluster with strength. We simply cannot let that happen as Americans.

Period.

Let me tell you what I literally tell every leader I've met with. Never, never, never bet against America.

Ordinary people like us, who do extraordinary things, we had candidates before attempting get elected by appealing to our fears, but they've never succeeded because we do not scare easily. We never bow. We never break when confronted with crisis. We endure! We overcome and we always move forward.

We are America, second to none, and we own the finish line!

— July 28, 2016

The Has-Been

IT'S NOT EASY TO IMAGINE BILL CLINTON AS THE FIRST LADY, but if Hillary is elected, he will be the oldest first lady in history.

Barbara Bush currently holds the title, having ascended to the post as George H.W. Bush's spouse at the age of 63. Bill will be seven years older. Michelle Obama used her time in the White House planting vegetable gardens and leading exercise classes. Bill is more likely to host senior golf tournaments and keynote the AARP convention.

America was a different country when Bill became president in 1993. There was no Twitter, no Facebook, no Google, no iPhone. If you wanted a portable phone, you had to buy a Motorola DynaTAC, which was about the size of a brick and offered 30 minutes of talk time for $4,000. If you wanted to send email, you used America Online. By the time he left office, you could Google "stained blue dress" and get the popular version of his presidency.

When Barack Obama needed a lift at the last Democratic convention in 2012, Bill Clinton stepped in to explain, in words even a white man could understand, how Obama was taking America to a better future. But he was here tonight not to look forward, but back.

"In the spring of 1971 I met a girl," he began. "She had thick blond hair, big glasses, wore no makeup, and she had a sense of strength and self-possession that I found magnetic."

Clinton recounted his many attempts to date her, then marry her, fleshing out along the way Hillary's own personal history. He told of going to her home in Park Ridge, Illinois, "a perfect example of post-World War II middle-class America, street after street of nice houses, great schools, good parks, a big public swimming pool, and almost all white." He met her crusty, conservative father, her rambunctious brothers and liberal mom.

Their courtship, by his telling, was hit and miss, as Hillary was always going off to pursue good causes: a summer internship interviewing workers in migrant camps; a trip to Dothan, Alabama, to end tax breaks for segregated schools; registering Mexican American voters in south Texas; researching the incarceration of black boys in men's prisons in South Carolina for prison reform legislation; finding disabled children shut out of schools in Massachusetts, writing up her findings in a report that would lead Congress to adopt the Americans with Disabilities Act. All in the span of two years.

On the convention floor, party whips handed out signs reading "Change Maker." But Bill wanted to get back to his love story.

"Meanwhile, let's get back to business. I was trying to convince her to marry me."

That happened on Oct. 11, 1975, in a little brick house with an attic fan and no air conditioning that he bought for her in Arkansas. And the rest is history, right? Not in a Bill Clinton speech. Old people like to reminisce.

His political career took him to Little Rock where his political ambitions led him from attorney general to governor, to ex-governor, to governor again. Along the way, they had little Chelsea Clinton.

"It was the greatest moment of my life. The miracle of a new beginning," he said. "For the next 17 years, through nursery school, Montessori, kindergarten, through T-ball, softball, soccer, volleyball and her passion for ballet, through sleepovers, summer camps and family vacations, from Halloween parties in the neighborhood to a Viennese waltz gala at the White House, Hillary first and foremost was a mother," he boasted.

In just over 50 words, Clinton gave his wife a dimension totally lacking in her campaign so far. A normal life. Not that it interfered with her political ambitions.

"She's insatiably curious, she's a natural leader, she's a good organizer, and she's the best darn change-maker I ever met in my entire life," he said.

Up with the signs.

Bill Clinton can riff on anything. When he's on a roll, there's no stopping him. His speech followed Chelsea to her freshman year at Stanford where he stood in a trance staring out the window while Hillary was "on her hands and knees desperately looking for one more drawer to put liner paper in." It was Chelsea who told them it was time to go.

"Now fast forward," he said, eliding a certain period when Congress impeached him, to Hillary winning a Senate race in New York and running for President in 2008.

Which brought him around to his point. How do you square what he just told you about Hillary and what you heard at the Republican convention?

"How do you square it? You can't. One is real, the other is made up. You just have to decide. You just have to decide which is which, my fellow Americans."

"If you win elections on the theory that government is always bad and will mess up a two-car parade, a real change-maker represents a threat," he went on. "So your only option is to create a cartoon. Cartoons are two-dimensional. They're easy to absorb. Life in the real world is complicated and real change is hard. And a lot of people even think it's boring."

There was so much in those last lines he could have gone on for another hour, but he was out of time. Alicia Keys was waiting in the wings, and Hillary was about to shatter the glass ceiling in a video marking her nomination to be the first woman President of the United States.

"Those of us who have more yesterdays than tomorrows tend to care more about our children and grandchildren," he concluded. "Your children and grandchildren will bless you forever if you do."

Think what you will about Bill Clinton, he still gives a good speech. But don't expect me to rush out to hear the next one at the AARP convention.

— July 27, 2016

One Man's Opinion

I wasn't much impressed by Hillary's speech last night. Over the last four days, a parade of citizens from all walks of life testified to Hillary's goodness and brought me around to thinking she's got this one in the bag. Then she stepped up to accept their nomination.

Of course, I hold her to a different standard than most of her followers. I'm a man. But I have my opinions.

Hillary's Problem

Men, especially white men, are Hillary Clinton's biggest problem. White men constitute around 34% of the electorate, and they are Donald Trump's biggest bastion of support. An early summer poll by ABC/*The*

Washington Post found Clinton trailing Trump by four points among white men with a college degree, and 14 points among those without.

It's easy enough for a man to come to a verdict on Trump. He's either a crazy motherfucker or he's going to make America great again. And we all know what that means: restore our manhood.

But there are a number of complicating factors to consider when a white man has to decide whether to vote for Hillary. First and foremost is her husband, Bill, whom we didn't much like in the first place.

For those old enough to remember, Hillary came into the public eye as the feisty spouse who wasn't going to just sit back and bake cookies like Tammy Wynette while the press pilloried her husband over his infidelities. She proved that when she lashed out at Bill's accusers during the Monica Lewinsky affair.

Privately she seethed at his stupidity, but she soldiered on and won a Senate seat in New York. We like that kind of grit.

Then she ran for President herself, losing out to Hope and Change in a primary battle against Barack Obama. Obama didn't get a majority of our votes. (57% of white males voted for John McCain.) But he won our respect. He played basketball. He told a good joke. He lifted America out of the greatest economic collapse since the Great Depression. And he appointed Hillary his secretary of state, which seemed like a gracious gesture at the time.

Her tenure as secretary of state complicated things. Yes, she visited some 112 countries representing the United States in dark days when Egypt, Tunisia, Libya, Syria, Gaza and Iraq were going through their Arab Spring. Obama got all the credit for the good things. Bringing our troops home, keeping nuclear weapons out of Iran's hands, hunting down bin Laden. And what did Hillary get credit for? Benghazi.

Bill Clinton and other speakers artfully threaded a new narrative through our collective memory at this convention. They told the story of the Hillary nobody knows, a woman who has dedicated her life to improving the lot of children, the disabled, immigrants, and, of course, women.

The best visual of the week was the moment when a photo of the 44 drab men who have occupied the Oval Office shattered to reveal her buoyant face on the Jumbotron. The female delegates swooned, cried and waved signs saying "History." Even the men had to admit it was a cool graphic.

Then President Obama set her up in one of those speeches only he can give. He endorsed her as the most competent man or woman to ever seek the office and eviscerated Trump like he was sliming salmon in Alaska. Bring on the nominee!

A Terrible Speech

In the Pantheon of great orators, Hillary's bust will never grace the main hall. She's given thousands of speeches, none of them memorable. She speaks in the cadence of a White house tour guide, with all the modulation of Siri reading the phone book. When she wants to make a point, she shouts. And she delivers an applause line like it's cold pizza in a cardboard box.

But her acceptance speech might have been one of her worst. Before the largest television audience she will have this election cycle—debates are another, but they let reporters into those—she wasted the opening five minutes thanking her daughter Chelsea for the introduction and Bill for conversations that filled her with joy in the good times (and "tested us" in the bad). She went on to thank Obama for his friendship, Joe Biden for, well, being Joe Biden, Michelle, Tim Kaine, Bernie Sanders, and young people in general.

"I've heard you. Your cause is our cause," she said. In her mind, that means making the Democratic Party platform happen.

Hold your breath and see if you can get through this paragraph without keeling over. She then outlined her plans for more jobs, higher wages, immigration, clean energy, gun control, drug addiction, mental health, prescription drugs, children with disabilities, money in politics, Flint's drinking water, climate change, profit sharing, a minimum wage, unfair trade deals, affordable health care, Social Security, small business, technological innovation, student debt, trade schools, family leave, income inequality, racial strife, voting rights, LGBT rights, worker rights, defeating ISIS, reforming the criminal justice system and building America's infrastructure.

The problem with a Hillary Clinton speech is she tries to cram in so many good causes they wind up smothering each other, and none get more than a sound bite of explanation. There is no arc to her narrative. Her speeches are bullet points taped together with bumper stickers like "Stronger Together" and "Love trumps Hate" and "Keep America Safe."

There were reports earlier in the week that Hillary was home fine-tuning the details of her speech. "It's true," she confessed. "I sweat the details." My suspicion is she was just shuffling the PowerPoint deck and practicing her pauses. Her big ideas are a lot of small plans that, as Daniel Burnham famously said, "have no magic to stir men's blood."

The Reluctant Feminist

I'm a man who came of age in the first wave of feminism. I read *Our Bodies, Ourselves* (and came away thinking those women sure know a lot more about their anatomy than we know about ours). I supported the women's movement in college, but I also supported the football team. We men are easy that way.

I admit I've been distracted by a woman's appearance, her smile and her willingness to put up with my jokes. That's part of the whole pheromone thing that keeps the human race going. But I never patted a woman's butt, or whistled as she walked past a construction site, or made her take a twirl in my office to get a job.

I never worked for a large company where unequal pay was built into the salary structure. I worked in the film industry—over, under, and alongside women—and we all thought we were underpaid. But I know the pay gap is real.

It wasn't until I had children and a wife with a job that maternity leave, day care, and women's health issues crossed my radar. Over time, I came to understand that the things boys take for granted—high school sports, military service, business opportunities—aren't available to girls in the same way.

So I get that Hillary was on to this early, and she not only brought it to the national conversation, she helped get something done about it. And her success fundamentally leveled the playing field in America.

But I have grown sons now who could care less. They are a key demographic in this election. Thirty-somethings, unmarried and focused on building their own careers.

They're not out-of-work steelworkers who painfully watched their factories go overseas. They're in the 95% of white men who are employed. (Though maybe not as gainfully as they, or I, might wish.) They too see a future in technology, clean energy, and innovative start-ups that will change America. But they also watch a lot of TV, and when they look at *The Apprentice*, they think to themselves, "Someday, I'd like to be that guy."

Earlier this week, I was talking with one of my sons about the convention, and he told me, "Enough of this woman stuff. What's she going to do for me?" And I don't think Hillary gave him any answers.

I like to think I'm more open-minded than that. I'm a man. I can live with complexity. I think making America better is a team sport, and I don't mind making a woman team captain. I just wish Hillary inspired me more. But I'll still probably vote for her.

Because the other guy is an asshole.

— July 29, 2016

2016 Election

Can We Talk?

LABOR DAY MARKS THE BEGINNING OF THE POLITICAL SEASON. Gluttons for punishment that we are, we ignore the billions of dollars candidates have spent branding their names on our foreheads and say we're ready to take this presidential race seriously now.

Ignoring what's already gone on is going to be hard this year. Donald Trump has commandeered the presidential stage, and his provocative personality has spread across the cable news channels so widely his hat should read "Make America My Next TV Show."

CNN has turned its newsroom into a game show studio where campaign shills sit on panels side by side with otherwise distinguished political commentators spewing out inane defenses of their candidate. Fox News has become the Trump network behind the fawning attention of Sean Hannity and Bill O'Reilly, and *Game Change* authors Mark Halperin and John Heilemann are giving MSNBC daily campaign news reports that they repackage into a Showtime series *The Circus* for the weekend.

Instead of polls, we're watching ratings. The overnights. What version of news were people watching last night? Why? Because if you're winning in the ratings, eventually you'll win at the polls, or so Trump would have you believe.

Old school political pundits prefer to go by the polls, and this year we've got a slew of them. Quinnipiac, Monmouth, Pew, Gallup, Rasmussen, YouGov, Marist, Reuters, Ipsos, Gravis, Suffolk. Take your pick. Anybody can randomly call 900 people, run them through an algorithm ("the secret sauce") and predict this race.

The pros check the polls like they are reading their daily horoscopes, paying particular attention to the crosstabs. How's a candidate doing with Blacks, Latinos, men, women, white women with a college degree, or white men with a toothpick stuck in their craw? It really doesn't matter. Election Day is two months off. The real campaign doesn't start until Labor Day. That's when people begin to talk about it.

All About Process

What distinguishes the campaign this year is the utter lack of issues. The cable news coverage is all about the process. Who's up in the polls, who's down, who has how much money (from whom), what swing states are in play, and, of course, who committed the biggest gaffe today on the campaign trail.

Donald Trump wins the gaffe contest hands down. In just the last few months, the Associated Press reports he has dissed 31 different racial groups, religions and perceived enemies. It's now common for the media to refer to Trump's campaign trail gaffes as "unforced errors." (We like our sports metaphors.) Trump changes campaign managers as often as Robin Ventura changes pitchers. A bad week on the campaign trail is called a slump. The play-by-play announcers count down the days until the game is over, and we stay glued to our seats like we are watching a pennant race.

How closely are we watching? Facebook reports that 100 million Americans have commented on the presidential race this year, generating 4 billion posts, likes and shares. The sad truth is we're all just talking to ourselves. We're divided into tribes; our friends are people like us. Like we have red states and blue states, we have Trump fans and Hillary fans. We watch the same news on different channels, Fox and MSNBC, and sometimes it's not clear they are even covering the same event.

In our social networks, we like the things we agree with, and rarely see the things we don't. Facebook has an algorithm that does that for us. According to a recent Pew Research Center report, 50% of Clinton fans have no close friends backing Trump, and 33% of Trump fans don't know any Hillary supporters.

No Common Ground

In the absence of common ground, the potential for misunderstanding is great. Trump and Clinton run around the country spouting buzzwords. For Trump, it's bad trade deals, dangerous immigrants and bad people who want to take away our guns. For Clinton, it's the environment, racial justice and income equity.

In our own little social networks, we get the gist of the race from all the blabber we hear on television and decide where we stand by seeing where all our Facebook friends are standing.

The Republican Party has become "an echo divorced from reality," Bret Stephens, a conservative commentator for *The Wall Street Journal*, says. The Democrats aren't much better. "We're not talking to each other, we're yelling at each other, but those on the other side of the gulf aren't listening," adds Charlie Sykes, a conservative radio host in Milwaukee. "We've basically eliminated any of the referees."

Trump Territory

I went out the other day to see my wife's brother Paul in Freeport, Illinois. This is Trump country. Paul runs an eye-opener bar that opens for the first shifts at the Newell Rubbermaid and Kelly-Springfield factories there and doesn't close until after the third shift leaves.

This year, Newell Rubbermaid and Kelly-Springfield are a shadow of what they used to be, and his business is off because his customers are off, permanently. Their jobs didn't ship out to China. Automation and conglomeration, not illegal immigration, reduced the number of workers needed on the factory floor, so the corporate honchos decided to consolidate their operations at fewer locations, making Freeport what sociologists call a "low-mobility" community.

There are fewer family businesses in town. Walmart and Target have moved in, and the small merchants along Main Street have closed up. The schools are good, but not great. Every year it's a struggle to pay the teachers. And an aging population has made health care a growth industry.

If you listen to the local scuttlebutt, you can't help but feel things are going to hell in a handbasket. Randy's wife attempted suicide in her kitchen, Dickie wrapped his car around a tree the other night when he was out drinking, and they just discovered a meth lab in a farmhouse on the outskirts of town.

"We're just moving along, same old, same old," Paul told me. "Except worse."

Paul is not a Trump voter yet. He thinks Donald Trump is crazy, but he still might vote for him. It won't be because he thinks Trump can solve Freeport's problems, it'll be because he has no confidence Hillary even understands them. Liberals seem to have a tin ear when it comes to understanding how small towns work. But conservatives are equally deaf to the difficult interplay of race, poverty, schools and crime in the inner city.

Can We Talk?

I long for the day when a politician would stop in at a local bar to talk to people, not just shake hands for a photo-op. When the issues would be talked about one topic at a time, where people would explain how things worked in their life, not get called on for a 60-second question in a CNN forum.

Instead, we are mired in yet another debate over Hillary's emails or Donald Trump's temperament. The warring camps throw tweets at one another that slide down the Twitter feed faster than a greased monkey.

What you think depends on what tribe you belong to, and the tribes are not talking to each other.

If you ask Paul if he thinks life in America was better 50 years ago, what do you think he will say? According to a Pew report, 81% of rural America says it was better in the old days, and 68% say they fear for their children's future.

The funny thing is if you ask the same question of parents in Chicago's inner city, you'll get the same answer. This is not good. We'd better figure out how we can work together to make both places better.

— August 30, 2016

Hate vs. Fear

SO THIS IS WHAT IT COMES DOWN TO, a choice between Hate and Fear.

It's not hard to fear Donald Trump. His interest in the presidency will end the moment he wins it. Oh sure, he's got a few ideas on how to redecorate the White House, and it'll be fun watching him negotiate a trade deal with his new best friends in Mexico.

But his ignorance of foreign policy is manifest. His people skills are nonexistent. He has no patience for dealing with those losers in Congress. There is nothing in the Constitution that lets him declare bankruptcy if his plan for America turns out as riddled with false promises as his casinos in Atlantic City. And God knows what he'll tweet out at 3 a.m. while he's up waiting for Putin to call.

If Trump wins, it will be because a vast swath of America yearns to break the gridlock in Washington, and they believe a brash businessman who once worked the halls of Congress for insider favors knows how to do that.

They are willing to overlook the fact he has nothing in common with them. He is a figment of their television imagination, the kind of guy they would be if only they had gotten a high school diploma, learned to play golf, or had a daddy with $100 million to invest in their business schemes.

Whether Trump wins or not, his base of supporters will have to be reckoned with in the next administration. They constitute some 40% of American voters, and they are not just disgruntled blue-collar workers in the Rust Belt. The preponderance are Republicans who've seen their incomes stagnate, their voices ignored and their influence diminished in an America that is becoming less white every day. They know Trump is a political charlatan, but they will "hold their nose" and vote for him. Why? Because they hate Hillary.

Likable Enough

Hillary Clinton is not an unlikable person. As Barack Obama famously said, she is "likable enough." But what makes her an easy target to hate is not her emails, her economic policies, or Benghazi. It's what she represents. Her story is baked into the Washington culture that Americans outside the Beltway disdain.

In a normal presidential election, Republicans and Democrats would have been discussing more conventional issues, offering up competing tax plans to stimulate the economy, different visions of America's role in the world, and new ideas for better health care, entitlement reform, educational opportunities, and job creation—all the things that matter, and nobody has the patience to work through.

Donald Trump's ascendance during the Republican primaries took a wide swing around the issues—good thing, since he doesn't understand them—and hopped along the steppingstones of hot-button grievances to what his supporters already felt in their hearts. The system is rigged against them.

Hillary Clinton is a product of that system. She's worked in every branch of the government, usually in the highest echelons of power, and attended all the embassy dinners, fundraisers and lobbyist soirees where big issues are discussed in side rooms. Everyone knows special interests are undermining democracy. She knows them by name. Never mind that she's opposed many of them. In the comity of Washington, everyone is friends. She even attended Donald Trump's wedding.

Her emails, the focus of so much Republican animosity, would be little more than a blip on the radar in a normal election, but they have come to define her. Exposing them was like pouring red dye into the system, revealing just how much public policy is actually conducted out of the public view. Do you really believe a secretary of state who has handled classified information for years and guarded the secret of the Bin Laden raid for six months would compromise American security through an act we all do every day? It beggars the imagination.

And yet, Trump rallies his troops with the cry "Lock her up!" for a scandal he calls bigger than Watergate. In any other election, this would all be a sideshow. But Trump has made it the centerpiece of his campaign because it taps into a rich vein of voters who think she is at the center of a government conspiracy against them.

The Washington press corps, particularly investigative reporters from *The Washington Post* and *The New York Times*, have done a bang-up job of covering the email imbroglio. But their influence is diminished by a plethora of other voices. Everyone has their own channel, their own take on things, and there is no reward for writing nuanced stories in a campaign that will be decided in the crucible of Hate vs. Fear.

Who Is the Media?

There will be a lot of seminars at the University of Chicago Institute of Politics next year assessing the media handling of this campaign. The first question to answer is what constitutes the media. In an era of declining print advertising, intense cable news coverage and surging alternative news sources, the notion of a mainstream media seems outdated.

In a single tweet, Donald Trump can reach 12.9 million followers on Twitter. Over 100 million Americans receive political posts on Facebook, and 25% of them say they rely on it. So it is especially concerning that most of them are reading, and sharing, posts from a constellation of like-minded people, all listening to the news and opinions they want to hear.

Somewhere in this political cacophony there have to be trend-setting news outlets, and that role seems to have fallen to CNN, Fox and MSNBC. Nothing could have worked out better for Trump. His experience on *The Apprentice* taught him how to work television's craving for showmanship, and his friendship with Roger Ailes guaranteed him unusual access to the Fox airwaves.

Before the campaign got under way, I attended an Institute of Politics seminar where Reince Priebus and Debbie Wasserman Schultz, the respective heads of the Republican and Democratic parties, reminded political reporters that the parties control the process. They run the primaries, hold the conventions, and put up the bulk of the money that pays for ads in the general election.

This year, Priebus said, Republicans will hold 12 primary debates, and the party won't tolerate unfriendly (read liberal) moderators. Fox News will wind up carrying five Republican debates, CNN four, ABC, CBS and CNBC, one each. (MSNBC was shut out.) And to get its debate slot, CNN had to promise to pair its moderator with a right-wing commentator from the Salem Radio Network. The days when the League of Women Voters dictates the terms are long gone.

Cable News or Entertainment?

The first debate on Fox, watched by 24 million people, broke all records for viewership. What should have been easy pickings for the Republican contenders quickly turned sour when Megyn Kelly, the moderator, asked Trump about calling women fat pigs, dogs, slobs and disgusting animals. The question—and Trump's response later that Kelly had "blood coming out her wherever"—set the tone for the campaign that would follow.

Trump survived the blow. He thrives on being politically incorrect. If anybody suffered, it was Kelly. She was pushed out of primetime and replaced by Sean Hannity, who soon turned his show into a Trump infomercial.

The man who learned the most from the first debate was Jeff Zucker, CNN's president. He had long coveted Fox's dominant news ratings, and he set out in 2016 to woo Fox's right-wing viewers by bringing more conservative commentators onto the CNN set. His signature mark on this election was pairing its regular panel of political commentators (David Gergen, Gloria Borger, David Axelrod, Jeffrey Toobin and Van Jones) with political shills from the campaigns—Donna Brazille and Paul Begala on the left; Jeffrey Lord, Kayleigh McEnany and Corey Lewandowski on the right—with Lewandowski receiving $500,000 for his appearances.

If the dialogue on the campaign trail were more substantive, there might have been a point to letting campaign surrogates expand on it. But Trump's defenders came armed with talking points for even his most outrageous ideas, believing (rightly, it turns out) that if they talked loud enough and long enough, they could run out the clock until the commercial break. Their blather only debased the political discourse and negated much of the good work CNN reporters were doing in the field.

I found myself this season gravitating to MSNBC for the intelligence of its commentators. Brian Williams, Chuck Todd, Chris Matthews and Rachel Maddow have their own clearly defined biases. But Nicolle Wallace was a welcome addition from the Republican side of the spectrum.

The Upshot

So we go to the polls this Tuesday with a very skewed perspective on the presidential choice we face. Lost in the media coverage is the fact America has never been as well off as it is today. Friday's unemployment number is 4.9%—lower than it has been in almost a decade. Hourly wages have risen 2.9% over last year. The country has seen 73 consecutive months of job growth in the private sector, and the annual deficit is $1 trillion less than it was in the first year of the Obama administration. That should bode well for the incumbent party.

Yes, there are pockets of poverty in America. The economy is still struggling with the effects of the Great Recession. There are questions about how to fix Obamacare, bolster our investment in infrastructure, reduce income inequality, make education more affordable, reduce crime in the inner city, preserve the environment, and assure that America maintains its leadership in the world.

We deserve a more rigorous examination of these problems and the candidates' solutions, not sound bites, often based on outrageously distorted facts. Instead, we get to cast our ballot against the person we fear most, or the person we hate most.

It's a sad end to a sad election. Nothing makes us feel Stronger Together or Great Again than an election that divides us.

— November 6, 2016

Down the
Rabbit Hole

Down the Rabbit Hole

As we descend down the rabbit hole into the Trump administration, let's harken back to a time when America was great. Two months ago.

Let's start with the latest February job numbers: 235,000 new jobs, or 4.7% unemployment. These are figures that Donald Trump once called phony but now thinks are fabulous.

Or how about a report from the Pew Research Center that shows 130,000 more Mexicans went back across the border in the last five years than came in. And he wants to build a wall?

Or a federal budget where health, education, the environment, science, compassion and lifting the hopes of the poor mattered. Now it's all about military spending and infrastructure.

When America was Great

When Donald Trump took office, the American economy was humming along quite nicely. From the depths of an economic collapse not seen since the Great Depression, the Dow Jones Industrial Average has risen from 7,950 points to 19,732. Job growth was up for the 76th month in a row, and 11.6 million more Americans are working than when President Obama took office.

On the world stage, U.S. troops in Afghanistan and Iraq fell from 200,000 in 2009 to 14,800 last year. This includes the 3,000 Special Forces assisting Iraqi forces fighting to regain control of Mosul and 900 more working with rebels in Syria. A third of Iraqi territory held by ISIS has been reclaimed, at a cost of fewer than a dozen American lives. And finally, we have a government in Iraq we can work with.

On the other side of the globe, after seven years of negotiations, the Obama administration forged a Trans-Pacific Partnership with 11 other nations that lowered trade barriers for one-third of the world economy. The wide-ranging agreement cut out 18,000 tariffs, recognized copyright, trademark and patent rights, cracked down on human trafficking, established workplace standards, set climate goals, and put America in the driver's seat for the next iteration of the global economy.

Then Donald Trump came along. He nixed it with an executive order on his third day in office.

Adjusting to Trump

I find it interesting how fast the media has adjusted to Trump's campaign rhetoric that Obama left him a mess. Suddenly, we are measuring our new president against Trump's campaign rhetoric and paying no heed to the legacy of goodwill his predecessor left him.

Never mind that his sloganeering—build a wall with Mexico, ban Muslims, take Iraq's oil, bomb the hell out of ISIS, make our allies pay more for their defense, and create more jobs, jobs, jobs—is jingoism at best, and unhinged from reality at worst. Trump is the new sheriff in town. He's crazy as a loon. And all the pundits on cable news can say is that we are in "unprecedented" times.

The Transition

The transition to a Trump presidency brought out all the flaws of our newly elected leader. He had no plan for a cabinet. He liked Rex Tillerson as secretary of state because he looked the part. He wanted Ben Carson for secretary of housing and urban development because he was black and grew up in Detroit. And who wouldn't want a defense secretary called "Mad Dog" Mattis? (Although Jim himself abhors the nickname.)

As to the rest of them? Well, that was up to Pence, his all-purpose stand-in for somebody who gives a damn. Last May, Trump named New Jersey Gov. Chris Christie to head up his transition team in the unlikely event he was elected. It was the least he could do for a man whose stone-faced mug has become an internet meme for shame. Christie's charge was to vet the potential appointees that Trump might name to fill the 7,200 political jobs that are awarded outside the civil service system.

Three days after he won, Trump replaced Christie with Pence because the process was moving too slowly. In the end, Trump would have the final word anyway. Between his photo-ops with Sean Penn and Kanye West, he took the high-profile candidates to lunch at 21, or Mar-a-Lago, or Trump National Golf Club. Just to get a feel for their game.

If somebody didn't work out, Pence was there to take the fall. So it's no wonder Pence somehow missed the letter from Rep. Elijah Cummings warning him five days after the election that Trump's choice for national security adviser, Gen. Michael Flynn, was being paid to lobby for foreign governments.

Trump had chosen Flynn himself. Then he was shocked (Trump speak: SHOCKED) to learn Flynn lied to Pence about his frequent phone calls to the Russians. The Senate Intelligence Committee is investigating whether Trump knew about them all along. If he didn't, why did he wait two weeks after the Justice Department ratted Flynn out to tell Pence?

Alice in Wonderland

There is a Lewis Carroll quality to Washington these days. More questions than answers. On the chessboard of politics, Trump is the Queen of Hearts. He rattles around the White House with a small coterie of advisers, barking out orders and constantly tweeting his opinion of everything.

In one early morning spurt, he accused the former president of the United States (four times) of wiretapping his campaign and still had enough venom left to ridicule Arnold Schwarzenegger for bungling his opportunity to host *Celebrity Apprentice*. In another tweet, he bemoaned Obama's release of 122 prisoners from Guantanamo (113 of whom were released by Obama's predecessor George Bush). In yet another, he huffed and puffed about a brutal terrorist attack in Sweden that never occurred.

I could go on, but why? There will be another tomorrow that is more outrageous than the last. Because Trump is convinced he can make public policy in 140-character bursts.

Like the Red Queen, he makes pronouncements on the spur of the moment. His legion of 26 million tweetees follow in lockstep, and he sends out his Jabberwockies to the cable news shows to defend, deflect or explain what he really meant. He believes what he believes is the best they can come up with.

Above it all, quietly nestled in the overhanging trees directing the narrative is his Cheshire cat, Steve Bannon.

Bannon's World

Bannon came late to the Trump campaign. A former investment banker at Goldman Sachs and head of *Breitbart News*, he was recommended to Trump by his financial mavens, Robert and Rebekah Mercer. They financed Bannon's last documentary "Clinton Cash" and were principal backers of Breitbart.

The unkempt political strategist and wide-tied candidate were not on the same page in the primaries. Bannon and Mercer were in the Ted Cruz camp. But when the Mercers switched their allegiance to Trump, Bannon came with them. Trump and Bannon quickly found common ground in their mutual delight poking fun at the mainstream media—and a shared disdain for the Washington establishment.

Bannon is not fazed by Trump's tweets, as long as Bannon remains in control of the narrative. For him, that narrative goes back to the 1400s when Western civilization was under attack by Islamic hordes. Two hundred years later, some Pilgrims left Europe for America, where freedom and prosperity flourished. Don't ask me how these two events are connected. But in the many documentaries Bannon has produced, the central themes are a) Islam is a threat to Western civilization and b) Big Government is the enemy of Free Enterprise.

Bannon's sway on public policy was first seen in Trump's executive orders —notably his ban on Muslim immigration—but it has reemerged in Trump's preliminary budget. As he proudly boasts, his ultimate goal is to "deconstruct" the federal government. Draconian cuts in every cabinet department, a slimmed-down foreign service corps and an eviscerated EPA are just warning signs. We're serious. You want to compromise, here's our starting point. Zero.

But you will never see Bannon defending these cuts in public. Like the Cheshire cat, he whispers his opinions in private conversations then disappears into the woodwork, and the last thing you see are his menacing eyes.

The Courtesans

The Red Queen's court is populated by sycophants and courtesans, otherwise known as Republicans in Congress. They are mum about Trump's erratic behavior because they need him to effect their agenda.

For years, House Speaker Paul Ryan has wanted to "repeal and replace" Obamacare and put more right-leaning judges on the Supreme Court. This week, as his health care bill comes to the floor, and Supreme Court nominee Neil Gorsuch goes before the Senate Judiciary Committee, he should be ecstatic. Instead, he's standing in front of the TV cameras twisting logic to explain what the President's last tweet actually meant.

With majorities in the House and Senate, and a Republican in the White House, overturning Obamacare should have been a walk in the park.

There isn't a Republican in Congress who didn't campaign against it (and even Democrats acknowledge there are ways to make it better).

What the Republicans didn't anticipate was the presidential candidate they put their money on didn't have the slightest idea what was involved. "Nobody knew health care could be so complicated." He kept spewing out pablum about how "everyone will be covered" and health care will be "better and cheaper"—a promise that Ryan knew Republicans couldn't fulfill—even though the Congressional Budget Office said 24 million more Americans will *not* be covered, and insurance premiums will *rise* 15 to 20%.

No Time to Be Right

Back when America was great, lobbyists battled over every nuance in Obama's Affordable Care Act. It took a year—and every trick in Nancy Pelosi's playbook—to pass, but 20 million more Americans wound up getting covered, and skyrocketing health costs were curbed.

Now, House Republicans are trying to undo it in six weeks. Tomorrow. From Ryan's perspective, it's now or never.

Why the rush?

Because in Donald Trump's America, there's no time to get it right. Only time to get it done. Trump is 50 days into his term. He has miles of promises to go before he gets through the first 100 days.

And who knows where his mind will be tomorrow.

— March 20, 2017

Impeachment:
How and When

IT TOOK RICHARD NIXON FIVE YEARS to lose the confidence of the American people. It has taken Donald Trump only two weeks.

President Nixon was impeached back in my day after his henchmen broke into the Watergate offices of the Democratic National headquarters, and he tried to cover it up. There were tapes recorded in the Oval Office that proved it. The idea a president would stoop to petty burglary to protect his presidency was enough to bring Arizona Senator Barry Goldwater and other prominent Republican officials to his doorstep to tell him it was time to step down.

The Emoluments Clause

But Donald Trump may be the first president to violate the Constitution even before he takes the oath of office. Other presidents have put their assets into a blind trust to steer clear of the emoluments clause in the Constitution. Donald Trump put his in the hands of his sons so he could beat the drum for his properties, and the whole family could profit. How? Check out the bookings at his Trump International Hotel in Washington during inauguration week. *Ka-ching.*

In olden days, emoluments were gifts intended to curry favor with the chief executive. Do room bookings from foreign diplomats, conferences and receptions at the Trump hotel in Washington or real estate deals in foreign countries count? You bet your sweet bippy.

Nobody has ever violated the emoluments clause so brazenly, so it has never been tested in court. But Richard Painter, President George W. Bush's top ethics lawyer, and Laurence Tribe, a Constitutional law professor at Harvard, have now joined a lawsuit to invoke it.

The Emoluments Clause (Article 1, section 9) states that no person holding any office of profit or trust "shall, without the Consent of the Congress, accept of any present, Emolument, Office, or Title, of any kind whatever, from any King, Prince, or foreign State."

In President Trump's mind, The United States is just another business in his portfolio of properties, and they all feed off the Trump brand. They're inseparable. *L'etat, c'est moi.*

High Crimes and Misdemeanors

The more traditional path to impeachment runs through Article II, section 4 of the Constitution where the grounds for impeachment are "treason, bribery or other high crimes and misdemeanors."

Trump was almost giddy when he discovered the president is exempt from conflict-of-interest statutes, but that immunity does not extend to bribery. If, for instance, a Saudi prince books 100 suites at Trump International, and the president shows his gratitude by giving him a $100 million F-35 jet, that's called bribery, or treason if it is deemed a betrayal of American interests.

But the most fertile grounds for impeachment are "high crimes and misdemeanors," a catch-all used three times to impeach Andrew Johnson in 1868, Richard Nixon in 1973 and Bill Clinton in 1998. Their crimes were, in order, not being Abraham Lincoln, masterminding a petty burglary, and getting a blowjob in the Oval Office. But high crimes and misdemeanors sounds more highfalutin.

The expression comes out of an English law dating back to 1386 under which officers of the Crown could be impeached for misappropriating government funds, appointing unfit subordinates, not spending money allocated by Parliament, or losing a ship at sea by neglecting to moor it properly. During the Constitutional Convention in 1787, the Founding Fathers debated whether to add corruption, maladministration, malpractice and neglect of duty, but decided "high crimes and misdemeanors" covered them all, and then some.

As his administration goes on, Donald Trump will no doubt commit one or more of these transgressions. But it is important to remember impeachment is not a legal proceeding. It is a political process subject to all the whims of public opinion and vagaries of politicians.

Building Momentum

Impeachment usually doesn't move forward until there is widespread agreement that the occupant of the Oval Office is a loose cannon. Widespread means Democrats *and* Republicans agree he is acting in an imperial manner outside the norms that the American people will accept.

While the federal courts weigh the constitutionality of Trump's ban on Muslim immigration, nearly half of the country—85% of Republicans—approve of it. His nomination of a conservative to the Supreme Court appealed to all segments of his party. There's a slim-to-none chance Republicans will want to do anything right now to upset the president while their agenda is moving through Congress.

Popularity

A baseline for measuring Trump's popularity today is his approval rating in the polls. When he took office, his approvals ranged from 48% in Gallup to 37% in Quinnipiac and 41% in the Real Clear Politics average. All are historically low measured against the 65% approval Presidents Clinton, Bush and Obama enjoyed when they took office.

How much further must Trump's approval fall before impeachment gets on the political radar? And are we really going by the polls? There are good reasons to be skeptical about the polls. They are easy to conduct, tainted by the phrasing of questions, subject to fungible algorithms, and the media reporting, especially on cable news, rarely unpacks the variation in responses from the South, Midwest and the coasts.

More to the point, Trump has no regard for them (unless they favor him). He will go to his grave believing his public support is as vast as the crowd at his inauguration.

No Fast Fix

Impeachment will not happen in the current session of Congress. To bring articles of impeachment, 24 Republicans would have to join all 194 Democrats in the House to vote for Trump's removal. And that would still comprise only the barest majority, not worth the political risk for leaders of either party.

Even if President Trump does something outrageous, the chairman of the House Judiciary Committee, where articles of impeachment must be drawn up, is Rep. Bob Goodlatte of Virginia who helped author Trump's Muslim immigrant ban this year and introduced legislation to abolish the House Ethics Office. But it's never too early to start the drumbeat.

Impeachment is a Process

President Trump thrives on being the center of attention. Does anyone believe he won't be front and center in the upcoming 2018 midterm elections?

His presence will loom over both House and Senate races. Just as Iraq overshadowed domestic issues in the 2006 midterm races, Trump's behavior will dominate this election. It may not make much difference in the Senate where Democrats will be defending 25 of the 33 seats up for grabs, but the House elections are a different story.

There's a good chance Democrats will pick up the 24 seats they need to regain control of the House, and Trump will fuel the outrage that does it. Theoretically, this puts the House in a position to impeach him. But that is only the first step. The trial will be held in the Senate where all 100 senators hear the charges, and 67 must vote to convict. Not bloody likely.

The Nixon Model

You might think a rational president would see the handwriting on the wall and step down, as Richard Nixon did. But Donald Trump is not a rational president. He will double down on his ability to fight off criticism with insults, false facts and braggadocio. A delegation led by Mitch McConnell himself could go to the Oval Office to ask Trump to resign, and they'd be pummeled with tweets as they left.

Impeachment is the process of coalescing public opinion around the need for urgent action. Reach across the aisle to talk to friends and family. Let's make it clear this presidency is not normal. Donald Trump is not only his own worst enemy, he is America's as well. It's time to start the process, knowing the outcome may not be all that we might wish.

— February 9, 2017

All in on The Wall

I'M GOING ALL IN ON THE WALL. If we're going to build the wall with
Mexico that Donald Trump has promised—"an impenetrable, physical, tall,
powerful, beautiful, southern border wall"—I don't want to be the last to
cash in. I'm going to invest in America's future. Concrete.

The task at hand is to wall off 1,954 miles of border with an impenetrable shield against illegal border crossings. Ten years of half-hearted
attempts by Congress have cost $2.4 billion and yielded only 650 miles of
barriers. Some are robust, like the 3.5-mile section that protects San Diego
from the terrorists gathering across the border. Most of the rest is wire
mesh, corrugated iron, or nothing at all because the surrounding terrain
prevents both fence builders and fence jumpers from getting there.

Congress, in its wisdom, has doubled the number of border patrol agents over the last 10 years from 10,500 to 21,000 agents. Trump has dismissed their efforts as little more than a catch and release program, but U.S. Customs statistics show border apprehensions as a result have dropped from a high of 1.6 million in 2000 to 400,000 in 2015.

But nothing says YOU ARE NOT WELCOME like a wall. So let's get down to it. How do we do that? A structural engineer in New York, writing under the pen name Ali F. Rhuzkan, outlined the challenge.

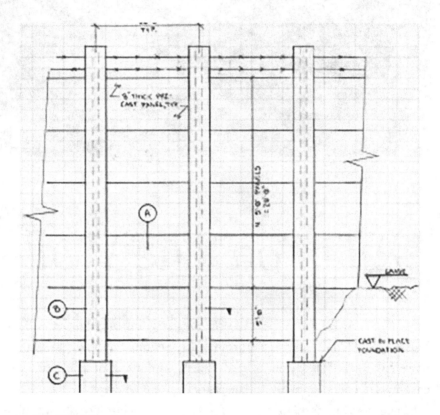

Chain link fencing is not feasible because it is easily breached with a simple wire-cutter. Cinder block is equally porous, and concrete cannot be poured on site because the process is too susceptible to temperature variations. The only viable solution is precast concrete panels held in place by iron pillars, Rhuzkan says. To deter tunneling, the wall should reach five feet underground and rise at least 20 feet above grade to discourage climbing.

Under the most straightforward design, assuming no deviations in the 1,954-mile path, he estimates the volume of concrete needed for the project would be:

- Foundation: 6 feet deep, 18-inch radius = 42.4 cubic feet
- Column: 4 square feet area by 30 feet tall = 120 cubic feet
- Wall panels: 25 feet tall by 10 feet long by 8 inches thick = 166.7 cubic feet
- Total concrete per 10-foot segment = 329.1 cubic feet
- 1,954 miles = 10,300,000 feet = 1,030,000 segments (10-feet long each)
- 1,030,000 segments @ 329.1 cubic feet per segment = 339,000,000 cubic feet = 12,555,000 cubic yards

So let's round that off to 12.6 million cubic yards: three times the amount of concrete used to build the Hoover Dam and greater in volume than all six pyramids of the Giza Necropolis in Egypt. That quantity of concrete could pave a one-lane road from New York to Los Angeles, going the long way around the Earth.

But that's only the start. When you add in the reinforcing rebar (roughly 3% of the total wall size), the additional iron required would be 10,190,000 cubic feet, or about 5 billion pounds. The cost of raw materials alone would come to about $17 billion, about the same the annual budget for NASA.

"But the challenge is far greater than simply collecting the necessary raw materials," Rhuzkan writes. "All of these hundreds of miles of wall would need to be cast in concrete factories, probably project-specific ones that have been custom built near the border. Then, the precast wall pieces would need to be shipped by truck through the inhospitable, often road-less desert. The men and women doing the work of actually installing the wall would have to be provided with food, water, shelter, lavatory facilities, safety equipment, transportation, and medical care, and would sometimes be miles away from a population center of any size. Sure, some people would be willing to do the work, but at what price? Would Trump hire Mexicans?"

In a news conference last August, Trump boasted to Univision's Jorge Ramos that building the wall would be "very easy."

"I'm a builder. That's easy. I build buildings that are—can I tell you what's more complicated? What's more complicated than building a building that's 95 stories tall."

What's more complicated is building that 95-story building sideways 5,400 times across America in the middle of a desert. It's all a pipe dream. But count me in. I can smell the meat a cookin'.

— November 15, 2016

The Salesman
in Chief

THE BEST SALESMEN SELL THEMSELVES. The product is what you get for liking them. And pay for.

That was no more evident than in Donald Trump's tweet the other day touting "our wonderful new healthcare bill" that he acknowledged, in the same breath, is subject to review and negotiation. Translation: Trust Me. It's gonna be great.

The bill cobbled together by House Republicans as the American Health Care Act, runs to a total of 66 pages—plus 57 pages of "reconciliations"—compared to the 906 pages in the original Obamacare bill it seeks to repeal. Does anyone really believe Trump has read it? This is a man who thinks getting through Dr. Seuss is like reading *War and Peace*—worth an "A" for effort.

Up to now, President Trump has left the crafting of his health policy to House Republicans because, as he admits, the repeal of Obamacare is a lot more complicated than he thought. Now he's ready to take the stage to sell it because, frankly, his surrogates have done a "C" job of messaging.

Junior Sales Associates

They are an odd bunch of junior sales associates still trying to learn the party line. As press secretary, Sean Spicer leads the pack. He almost didn't make it through his first week after appearing at his first official press conference to explain Trump's false claims about his inauguration crowds (or lack of them).

To be fair, Spicer didn't have much to work with. Photos comparing Obama's inauguration crowds and Trump's, as well as D.C. Metro ridership numbers, belied the claim. When he finished, Trump privately laid into him for wearing a bad suit.

It has gone downhill for Spicer ever since (although he did get a better suit). He has tried various tactics to soften questioning from the White House press corps. He switched around the press seating, padded the assemblage with alt-right news reporters, accused the media of being an enemy of the people, and banned TV cameras from his gaggles.

Trump's latest salvo accusing President Obama of wiretapping his campaign tested Spicer to the limits. For three days, he dissembled before the press. Finally, he was asked if he *personally* had seen evidence support-ing Trump's claim.

"That's above my pay grade," he answered. "I'm not here to speak for myself. I'm here to speak for the President of the United States and our government."

The Yo-Yo Corps

Meanwhile, the White House has yo-yoed other spokespeople into the TV talk shows to make the president's case. Kellyanne Conway proved such an unreliable vehicle for the truth that CNN and *Morning Joe* temporarily banned her.

Boris Epshteyn, a combative Trump loyalist with the title special assistant to the president, quickly made himself persona non grata at the networks, according to *Politico,* by getting into a yelling match with a Fox News booker and threatening to keep all West Wing officials off their air.

"He calls women girls, and he has no decorum about how he speaks to people," Joy-Ann Reid, an MSNBC national correspondent, told *Politico.* "He's somebody that just makes the room uncomfortable. When he leaves the room, the conversation is, 'I hope he never comes back.' He enjoys making people uncomfortable."

For the wiretap tweet, the White House trotted out Mike Huckabee's daughter Sarah Sanders, now deputy press secretary, where, on ABC's *Good Morning America*, George Stephanopoulos admonished her *three times* that what she was saying "is simply not true."

And then there is Stephen Miller, the 31-year-old senior policy adviser to the president who crafted much of his first speech to Congress. Last February, Miller made the rounds of Sunday talk shows spouting unsubstantiated nonsense with such supercilious certainty he looked and sounded like Hitler's Minister of Propaganda Joseph Goebbels.

"Congratulations Stephen Miller—on representing me this morning on the various Sunday morning shows," Trump tweeted. "Great job!"

Messaging or Message

The biggest problem the White House faces isn't the messaging, it's the message. Trump often sets the tone for the day with 6 a.m. tweets that veer off into bonkers land. Even when he is on message, Twitter allows only 140-character posts (unless Trump is in a tweet storm) so his mind swirls around in cliches. We must protect our borders, bring back jobs, get rid of Obamacare. Sad. Terrible. MAGA.

The Republican health care bill poses a challenge to the whole way Trump thinks about issues. If he read it, he would find its 66 pages are filled with more air than answers: who is covered, who is not, how do subsidies for low-income earners compare to Obamacare's, what is the effect on standard insurance rates, what procedures are not covered, how will it impact drug pricing, or state Medicaid programs? And critically, what will it cost? (The Congressional Budget Office has yet to score the bill.)

As he steps forward to lead the charge, don't expect Trump to provide those details. He is not, as Obama was, the explainer in chief. He is the salesman in chief.

All About the Brand

In a Trump White House, it's all about the brand. The shine on the apple. The veneer of significance. If you look at his long career in business, it's always been that way. Whether he's selling wine, steaks, hotels, university degrees, golf courses, ties, casinos or condominium towers built by someone else, he's selling a Trump. And now we have Trumpcare.

It's his name on the door, so like all good salesman, he wants to make sure the product is prime rib, or, if it's a piece of crap, none of that crap sticks to his shoes.

Lessons from *The Apprentice*

His penchant for gilding the lily started early in his New York real estate career. His craving for celebrity had him calling society columnists using a fake name to plant stories about himself. But it reached its apogee in the hit TV show that launched his political career.

The *Apprentice* was a clever piece of TV stagecraft: The boardroom and a penthouse suite where contestants supposedly stayed were Hollywood sets built into Trump Tower. Contestants advanced or were fired based on whims and petty disputes. Hundreds of hours of raw tape were edited down every week into a narrative where Trump was the ultimate decider. Mark Burnett, the executive producer, developed the technique in *Survivor*, but Trump meticulously monitored the final version to make sure he was always portrayed in the best light.

He took the same liberty in promoting the show as he did as its star. On the campaign trail, he called it the #1 hit on television when, in fact, the highest rated episode (the finale to season one) came in seventh, and the last 10 years of *Celebrity Apprentice* fell into the middling range of 46th to 84th.

'Full Sell Mode'

On Wednesday, Spicer told a press conference the White House will be putting on "a full-court press" to get the Republican health care plan passed in the House next week.

"We are out in full sell mode all around the country, talking about how we think this is the best way to solve the problem that the American people face and why we believe that the solutions that we put forward in this bill are the right ones and that will benefit them," he said.

All the Trump surrogates will be out in force on cable news, local TV stations and the radio talk shows. Who do you suppose gets Kellyanne and who gets Goebbels? Trump himself is also taking an active role. He's meeting with key congressmen, saying nice things on Twitter about people he loathes, and, according to Spicer, he's eager to get back on the road barnstorming for the Republican plan.

Let's Make a Deal

Spicer would not commit to making Trump himself available to the press to answer questions that have been pouring in from an array of opponents that includes the American Medical Association, the Catholic Health Association, American Nurses Association, American Hospital Association, Children's Hospital Association, AARP, Club for Growth and the entire Democratic Party.

That's a lot of stakeholders who will have to come together before Obamacare is repealed or replaced. But Spicer likes the boss's chances. "If anybody can get a deal on something, it's Donald Trump."

Except, ultimately, of course, it's not whether you can make a deal that matters, it's what kind of deal you make.

— March 9, 2017

The Environment Is Overrated

I LIVE IN CHICAGO. Our summers are too hot. Our winters suck. You never know what week in the fall the leaves will actually fall. And you can be picking Easter eggs out of snowbanks in the spring.

What's all this fuss about climate change? It's just the weather out of control again. Isn't it?

Climate Change

Our understanding of weather patterns has grown immensely in the last 50 years. Satellite technology has given us new insights into the fragile ozone layer surrounding the earth. Research centers around the world have taken the data, mapped it along historical timelines and determined that carbon dioxide emissions, primarily generated by cars, trucks, factories and power plants, are wreaking havoc on the greenhouse gases that protect our planet.

On television, we see the evidence in ice cliffs falling into the sea off Greenland, New York subways flooding during Hurricane Sandy, and deadly tornados ripping through the Midwest. But that's what television does, puts the face of disaster right in our living rooms.

There are voices in the alt-right news ecosystem with a different view. They believe all of this talk about climate change is a hoax perpetrated by the Chinese to keep America from exploiting our bountiful coal, oil and natural gas resources.

Unfortunately, one of them is our president.

Rolling Back Obama's Eco-Legacy

In a bizarre ceremony Tuesday at the headquarters of the Environmental Protection Agency, President Trump issued another executive order rolling back a host of EPA regulations issued under the Obama administration. All were aimed at meeting America's pledge to reduce its carbon dioxide emissions 26% by 2025, our contribution to a better environment under the Paris climate accord.

But Trump said nothing about the pact itself, or the environment, or his own views on global warming. His message was jobs, jobs, jobs. David Roberts, the environment reporter for *Vox*, eviscerated the speech as "a sprawling mess…comically plutocratic…seared with a thick sheen of populist rhetoric…a scattershot and utterly unmotivated policy, rooted in deep scientific ignorance, enriching a small set of fossil fuel executives on the basis of no coherent policy rationale." Don't sugarcoat it, Dave, what did you really think?

Coal Takes Center Stage

When the Paris Agreement was signed in 2016 (by 194 nations) President Obama faced a hostile Congress, so he used the EPA's regulatory authority to create what he called a Clean Power Plan. The coal industry, which over the last five years has been steadily losing market share to cheaper natural gas prices, would bear the brunt of it.

The EPA orders prevented mines from dumping sludge in nearby rivers and waterways, required expensive retrofits in dozens of coal-fired power plants and made construction of new ones all but impossible. Obama put a moratorium on new coal leases on federal land and ordered oil and gas companies to plug the methane leaks in their field operations.

Together, all of these would have met our Paris commitment, he said, while smarter conservation efforts and surging renewable energy sources kept the economy humming. But the new president was having none of it.

"My administration is ending the war on coal," he said. "We're going to have clean coal. Really clean coal. Together we will create millions of good American jobs, also so many energy jobs, and really lead to unbelievable prosperity."

Trump made the announcement in a room filled with coal miners. He held the executive order high in the air after he signed it. "You know what this is? You know what this says?" he beamed. "You're going back to work."

Except...

Except that's not what it said at all. It was an executive order that directed his EPA to write new regulations undoing Obama's old regulations through one of the most politically charged rulemaking procedures in Washington.

It took the Obama administration two years to get the Clean Power Plan regulations approved. It will take that long and more—with many stops along the way in the federal courts—for Trump's replacement to get through, predicts Mark Barteau, director of the Energy Institute at the University of Michigan.

"The only people who are going to get jobs out of this are lawyers," he said.

A Little Bit of History

The EPA was created by Richard Nixon in the hippy-dippy '70s when Earth Day was an occasion to send Boy Scout troops out to pick up beer cans along the highway.

A year before the EPA came into existence, Congress passed the National Environmental Protection Act to "create and maintain conditions under which man and nature can exist in productive harmony." On signing the act, Nixon declared that 1970 would be the year "when America pays its debt to the past by reclaiming the purity of its air, its waters, and our living environment."

The dirty job of doing that would fall to the EPA. Its task was to handle all the things none of the other federal departments wanted to take on: air pollution, water quality, garbage dumps, smokestack emissions, pesticides, industrial waste, poisonous chemical leaks, endangered species and recycling programs.

Over the next four decades, Congress would add to the list in an array of bills with high-minded titles like the Clean Air Act, the Clean Water Act, the Safe Drinking Water Act, the Oil Pollution Act, the Toxic Substances Control Act and the Superfund clean-up. But money to enforce them was rarely attached.

New Frontiers

Each took the EPA into new frontiers in environmental science. Just to set standards, it had to organize science labs, issue research grants and collaborate with college and university science departments. It set up a national network of testing stations to monitor air and water quality and funneled the raw data into arcane computer models that might, over time, yield real-world solutions.

Writing the regulations was always a delicate balance between the nation's economic and environmental interests. Scientists offered complicated explanations for the benefits of a particular EPA rule; the industries affected countered with arguments about jobs lost or customers ill-served. Public interest groups weighed in during the comment period. Hearings were held. Then more comments, and the congressmen who hold the purse strings of the EPA budget were always weighing in on behalf of constituents, or special interests.

Where the EPA invariably got in trouble was the last mile of the process, enforcement. To stretch an already thin budget, the EPA has forged partnerships with state environmental protection agencies, which handle much of the permitting and inspection duties. But when an air-conditioner repairman can't use freon anymore, or a farmer gets a citation because his cow manure is flowing into Brown's Creek, or a developer incredulously asks why he has to file an environmental impact statement, the blame falls on the EPA.

The Rare and Endangered Snail Darter

It was only three years after the EPA was created that it became embroiled in its first controversy. In 1973, a scientific researcher found a school of rare but endangered snail darters living in the shallows next to a dam under construction on the Little Tennessee River. The Endangered Species Act made saving the fish, no bigger than bait, a priority over all federally funded projects. The construction was halted. The Tennessee Valley Authority took the case to court, and the Tellico Dam—already 99% complete—sat idle for five years until the U.S. Supreme Court in 1978 reaffirmed the fish's inalienable right to exist.

With half of the Tennessee Valley waiting on the 200 million new kilowatt hours of hydroelectric power the dam could deliver every year, Sen. Howard Baker took to the floor of the Senate to ask his colleagues for a new bill exempting the Tellico Dam from the act.

"I have nothing personal against the snail darter. He seems to be quite a nice little fish, as fish go," he said, but "the snail darter has become an unfortunate example of environmental extremism, and this kind of extremism, if rewarded and allowed to persist, will spell the doom of the environmental protection movement in this country more surely and more quickly than anything else." The bill sailed through, and the dam opened in 1979.

The Attack on the EPA

Once the photo-op at EPA headquarters was over, President Trump moved on to his next event, a White House reception for senators and their wives to repair his frayed relations with Congress.

The hard work of dismantling the agency now lies in the hands of his new director, Scott Pruitt, the former Oklahoma attorney general who made a career out of suing the EPA—11 times—over oil and gas regulations.

The knives have been out for the EPA since early in the Trump transition. In March, Mick Mulvaney, the new director of the White House Office of Management and Budget, unveiled a Trump budget blueprint that will slice 31% from the EPA budget and lay off 20% of its staff. The total workforce will go from 15,376 to 12,176, half of whom are scientists, engineers and environmental researchers.

"You can't drain the swamp and leave all the people in it," Mulvaney told reporters. "The president wants a smaller EPA. He thinks they overreach, and the budget reflects that."

In fact, the EPA is already the smallest cabinet-level department in the government. Its annual budget of $8.1 billion compares to $580 billion for the Defense Department. But while the Trump administration is planning to give the Pentagon another $54 billion, it is taking $2.4 billion away from the EPA.

Other Budget Cutbacks

The Environmental Protection Network, a group of former EPA employees and policy experts, has issued a 50-page analysis of the Trump budget blueprint that details other cuts to long-standing programs:

- The Office of Science and Development will be slashed 48%.
- Compliance and enforcement funding will be cut 23%.
- Clean air, water and waste management programs will be cut 10% to 35%.
- Grants supporting state environmental protection agencies will be slashed 45%.
- Funds for long term, multistate initiatives to clean up the Great Lakes, Chesapeake Bay, the Florida Keys, San Francisco Bay, Puget Sound and the South Florida ecosystem will be eliminated. In the case of the Great Lakes, which hold 21% of the world's fresh water, this amounts to a loss of $300 million a year.

- The Energy Star program encouraging energy-efficient appliances will be eliminated.
- Periodic reports on the impact of climate change and 33 other indicators (temperature, sea level, Antarctic sea ice, flooding and drought) will be discontinued.
- Overall funding to clean up hazardous waste at Superfund sites will drop from $1.1 billion to $762 million, a reduction of 30%.

And that just scratches the surface. Hundreds of other lesser-known EPA initiatives are being stripped to the bone in what amounts to a scorched earth approach to the environment.

Taking the Good with the Bad

It's easy to grouse about the inconvenience of EPA regulations, but let's not forget the good things that have come out of it.

Without the EPA, urban smog would not be down 84% in our major cities. Lead paint would still be used in home construction. Smart appliances with an Energy Star label would not be saving consumers $14 billion a year on their energy bills. And new cars would still be chugging along at 9 miles per gallon instead of the federally mandated 24.8.

There would be no rapid response team for oil spills in the Gulf or emergency plan for radiation leaks at nuclear plants. Thousands of acres of abandoned factories on brownfields filled with toxic industrial waste would not have been returned to public use. Flint, Michigan, might still be drinking poison water. And I'll bet you dimes to donuts, without the EPA's Great Lakes program, we'll be seeing Asian Carp dive-bombing the boats off Navy Pier in a few years.

Save the 18th Hole

President Trump is not one to get bogged down in the weeds of science, but he does have a few opinions on the environment—shaped by his ownership of golf courses around the world. Two ongoing disputes with local officials, in particular, show he can take either side of the climate change debate.

In Scotland, he's fighting tooth and nail against wind turbines that spoil the view from the clubhouse of his Aberdeen golf course. He's serious about it. He's tweeted 60 times on the subject. "When I look out of my window and I see these windmills, it offends me," he told Britain's Nigel Farage just after the election. "Let's put them offshore. Why spoil the beautiful countryside."

Meanwhile in Ireland, he's all for building a seawall on the dunes in County Clare to protect his Trump International Golf Links & Hotel in Doonbeg. In 2014, an Atlantic storm washed away the 18th hole, and the Trump Organization has spent $60 million restoring the property.

To protect its investment, it tried to remedy the problem by hauling massive boulders into a marshy spot next to the hotel. Now it is proposing now a 13-foot seawall weighing 200,000 tons that will run 1.7 miles along the dunes. But the local county council has halted the project. Let Caelainn Hogan, writing in *The Guardian*, explain.

"Trump's wall was thwarted by the tiny, narrow-mouthed whorl snail, which lives in the dunes. The snail, around since the ice age but now endangered, is protected in Ireland, and binding conditions in the original planning permission demand regular monitoring to ensure activities on the golf course do not endanger it."

Local residents have organized against the wall on the grounds that erosion is a natural part of the dune's dynamic ecosystem. They are concerned the seawall will redirect the water into low lying farms just to the south. And besides, Doonbeg is no place for a golf course.

Coal Country

The heyday of coal has come and gone. In 1923, there were 863,000 miners climbing down the shafts to bring out the black gold that fueled an industrial revolution. Today, that number has dwindled to 65,400.

The coal-fired plants Obama wanted to close supply about 33% of America's electrical power. Natural gas is cheaper, with nuclear plants and hydroelectric dams supplying the rest. But all the action these days is in the wind and solar arena. While coal is in decline, the solar power industry has added 374,000 new jobs to the economy, according to the Department of Energy.

Even coal company executives don't lay all the blame for coal's decline on the EPA's doorstep. More damaging to the bottom line has been weak exports to China, lower prices from domestic shale gas and the growth of renewable energy sources.

On NPR, which is doing an excellent job of staying in touch with Trump voters in the hinterlands, a housewife in eastern Kentucky said everyone knows the coal mining jobs are never coming back, but she loves Trump because he stands up for them.

Another Trump political rally at EPA headquarters is not going to keep the climate from changing. If the planned budget cuts to EPA go through, we'll have a lot less hard evidence about how—or how fast.

Sure, every federal agency can use a good scrubbing. But that's no excuse to throw out the baby with the bathwater. Let's let the EPA researchers do *their* jobs. Somebody has to care about the environment—because the president sure doesn't.

Unless, of course, some duffer takes a divot at Trump International and discovers a rich vein of black gold running under the 5th fairway. Then, Johnny, grab a shovel. All bets are off.

— March 31, 2017

Trump's First 100 Days

WE SHOULD ALL BREATHE A SIGH OF RELIEF that the government
will not be shutting down this weekend because that will give us more time
to prepare for the nuclear war.

The drumbeats of war were muffled this week as the Trump administration was marching to a different drum, a celebration of its first 100 days
in office. Thirty members of the Trump brain trust met in the Executive
Office two weeks ago to figure out how to cram as much fluff into Trump's
record as the good ship Almost True could hold. The first out to spread
the good news was Kellyanne Conway appearing on CNBC to tout the fact

Trump is the only president to ever get a Supreme Court judge approved in his first 100 days. (To a vacancy Merrick Garland should have filled a year ago.)

Sean Spicer then took a swing at legacy building in the White House press room with a tally of executive orders Trump has issued, congressional bills he's signed and foreign leaders he's talked to. "When you look at the totality of what we've accomplished…it is unbelievable what he has been able to do," Spicer said.

Many of those executive orders, of course, were directives for more study. The 28 congressional bills Spicer cited included 13 rescinding Obama's executive orders, two renaming post offices, and one urging more people to fly the flag on Veterans Day.

Trump himself kicked off legacy week with a tweet. "No matter how much I accomplish during the ridiculous standard of the first 100 days & it has been a lot…media will kill me!"

Many Ways to Say Not Good

He wasn't far off the mark. Most reporters in the mainstream media were generous in their assessment, framing their first 100 days stories in terms of campaign promises kept. The recurring theme was that the man known for the art of the deal has so far shown he can't make a deal. He couldn't get through a new health care law, fund a border wall or wheedle his way out of the Russia meddling investigation.

His presidential transition had been chaotic. His first choice for national security adviser Michael Flynn was drummed out of office for lying to the vice president. Hundreds of key administration slots requiring Senate approval go unfilled. And there's an ongoing war among his top advisers Steve Bannon and Jared Kushner for his attention.

Not to put too fine a point on it, reporters who work in the White House every day seem to have taken cover under the blanket description of Trump's first 100 days as unprecedented (or "unpresidented," as he puts it).

This Is Not Normal

But Michael Grunwald of *Politico* didn't pull any punches when he offered this analysis.

"The indelible takeaway from his first 100 days is that Trump's assault on political norms...has violated Washington norms so casually and constantly that his norm-breaking is becoming normalized," he wrote. "Some of Trump's *he-did-what?* provocations have been consequential in their own right, like his explosive accusation that President Barack Obama wiretapped him, which he refused to retract even after it was debunked, or his conspiracy theory about 3 million illegal voters, which many see as a prelude to a push to restrict voting rights.

"He's flouted democratic norms with banana-republic attacks on journalists, judges, protesters, the Congressional Budget Office and other critics beyond his control. He's flouted anti-corruption norms by refusing to divest his business empire, spending almost every weekend at his own clubs, and making little apparent effort to avoid conflicts of interest. He's defied the Washington hypocrisy police with incredibly brazen flip-flops on Syria, Medicaid cuts, China, NATO, Goldman Sachs and the nefariousness of presidential golf. And even though he had no experience in government, he's shocked Washington by surrounding himself with aides who have no experience in government: his son-in-law, his daughter, the former head of a right-wing website and a Goldman executive.

"In general," Grunwald concluded, "the story of his first 100 days has been a words story, not a deeds story, an embarrassing contrast to Obama's action-packed early presidency. Trump has seized control of the national narrative and taken up residence in the national headspace, but he hasn't put much of a stamp on federal law, federal rules or the federal bureaucracy. So far, he's been a show horse, not a workhorse, and in Washington, show horses often struggle to produce lasting change."

A Tornado of Activity

With only four days left in Legacy Week, the White House suddenly found more significant achievements than it knew what to do with. Treasury Secretary Steven Mnuchin started the day off at the White House by unveiling a package of recycled campaign promises he called "the largest tax cut in history." The federal tax code runs to 74,608 pages. Mnuchin's proposal was 12 points on a single sheet of paper, double-spaced.

The point of it all, clearly, was to give Trump another box to check off in his first 100 days. Proposed huge tax cut. Check. The president, meanwhile, was over at the Department of the Interior signing an executive order to roll back a ban on oil drilling in newly designated national monuments. Boost oil production. Check. From there, he moved on to the Department of Education to sign another executive order affirming his administration's commitment to keeping the federal government out of local schools. Save local schools. Check.

While he was out checking the boxes, White House aides floated a story to *Politico* that the president was about to sign an executive order pulling the U.S. out of the NAFTA. When word got around, the Mexican peso and Canadian dollar plummeted. On his return to the White House, Trump found Mexican President Enrique Pena Nieto and Canadian Prime Minister Justin Trudeau on the phone bewildered.

By nightfall, the White House issued a statement clarifying that, instead of ending NAFTA, all the parties would sit down to renegotiate it. What did I say about Trump with a cell phone? The next morning at 6:12 a.m. Trump was back on Twitter warning the negotiations were "subject to the fact that if we do not reach a fair deal for all, we will then terminate NAFTA."

Meanwhile, in the Real World

Secretary of Defense James Mattis meanwhile was briefing senators on the dangerous situation developing in North Korea. While the president was polishing his apple, a Navy armada was steaming toward Korea and parading a nuclear submarine through South Korean waters in response to North Korea firing an intercontinental ballistic missile 4,000 miles into the Pacific Ocean.

No shrinking violet himself, North Korean dictator Kim Jong Un released a frightening video that depicts an all-out attack on America and followed that with a massive live fire demonstration of his heavy artillery along the DMZ. The threat of a war with North Korea over its nuclear program is very real. Relying on the Chinese government to rein in Kim Jong Un is a pipe dream.

Trump solemnly warned that "all options are on the table," but he did in a such a way it sounded like we're going to throw a lot of options at North Korea and they'll buckle under the weight.

I wish President Trump had spent less time this week worrying about his legacy and more time reading the intelligence reports. This is one of those moments when the judgment, stability and experience of the man in the Oval Office matters, and nothing in these first 100 days gives me confidence he has them.

"The Trump presidency often feels like reality TV. But this is reality," Grunwald wrote. "His current showdown with North Korea is a real showdown. His painfully awkward meeting with German Chancellor Angela Merkel was a real meeting. His news conference where he described his rookie-run, blood-feuding White House as a "fine-tuned machine.... was a real news conference."

In the real world, it matters whether our president has a strategy, and whether he has thought through that strategy to all its possible conclusions, good and bad.

Because there are no mulligans in a nuclear missile attack, no chocolate cake desserts in the Situation Room and no Chapter 11s if something goes awry. This moment will be President Trump's real legacy.

— April 28, 2017

BREAKING NEWS

WH DEFENDS SHIFTING STORY ON COMEY FIRING

Initially said it was Deputy AG's idea; Trump now says it was hi...

The National Conversation

DAVID BROOKS AND E.J. DIONNE were on NPR the other night talking about the chaos of the last two weeks in Washington. Inevitably, their thoughts turned to Watergate. "I'm old enough to remember," Dionne recalled. "It seems to me this story is moving so fast it's like we're in the last days of Watergate, and Trump has only been in office 120 days."

On the journalistic front, it feels good to be back. It's heartening to watch *The Washington Post* and *New York Times* in a good old-fashioned newspaper war over who has the latest, and deepest, sources in the Russian investigation. It's comforting to see congressional committees investigating high crimes and misdemeanors, not cleaning out Trey Gowdy's sock drawer of smelly inferences. And it's fun to flick around the TV dial to monitor the national conversation on three cable channels that weren't in existence back in the Watergate era.

A Cacophony of Voices

The national conversation is a term that journalists use to burnish their role in society. Originally, it was conducted on the editorial pages of the nation's great newspapers, or in opinion journals like *The Nation, The New Republic* or *National Review*. The mass audiences that flocked to television in the '60s made the nightly network newscasts a focal point during the Vietnam War and Walter Cronkite "The Most Trusted Man in America." Over time, CNN and the other cable news channels joined the fray. Rush Limbaugh, with his audience of 14 million listeners, showed that talk radio deserved a place at the table, and then came the Internet, which unleashed a cacophony of voices.

The Disruptive Force of the Internet

One explanation for Donald Trump's success in the last election is the disruption the Internet brought to that conversation. Newspapers reeling from declining readership and revenues had little effect on the election outcome. Ninety-eight of 100 major papers endorsed Hillary Clinton, and Trump still won. The TV airwaves were so saturated with vitriolic speeches and specious claims, there was no time to get to the bottom of an issue.

The digital frontier that spawned *Politico* and *PolitiFact*—the fact-checking website that won the first Pulitzer Prize for digital reporting—also gave us *The Drudge Report, Breitbart* and *InfoWars*, not to mention a host of fake news postings on Facebook and Twitter planted by Russian intelligence agencies.

The schizophrenia in the electorate was mirrored in the three cable channels. Roger Ailes went all in for Trump on Fox News; MSNBC deployed a bevy of hard-charging young correspondents to dog Hillary Clinton on the campaign trail, and CNN reconfigured its studio set to let surrogates for the candidates have their say. Everyone, it seemed, had an opinion, sometimes based on facts, sometimes based on alternative facts.

In the mind of the man who ultimately benefited from all this confusion, President-elect Trump, the jockeying for relevance was the last gasp of a failing media elite. He mocked the "dishonest" media and called them "the enemy of the people" at his rallies. What did he need them for anyway? He had Twitter and 27 million followers.

The First 100 Days

Last week, Harvard's Shorenstein Center on Media, Politics and Public Policy issued a report on media coverage of Trump's first 100 days in office. To no one's surprise, it was overwhelmingly negative.

Eighty percent of the news stories had a negative tone, according to the report, compared to 60% negative for Bill Clinton in his first 100 days, 57% for George W. Bush, and 41% for Barack Obama (although Obama's rating turned 57% negative in his next 100 days).

Tucked inside the favorable/unfavorable numbers are some unique insights into how the press is covering Trump. In the first 100 days, he was the topic of 41% of all TV news stories—three times more than other presidents—and 65% of the TV talk was by Trump himself.

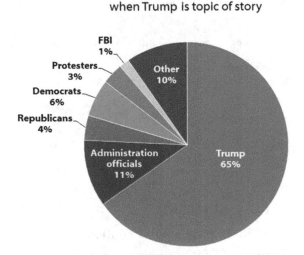

percentage of TV talking time
when Trump is topic of story

The cable news channels are "All Trump, All the Time," the report states, providing 24/7 coverage that amounts to 200 hours of Trump mania a week, every week, streaming into American living rooms. And viewers are eating it up.

"You have to be in a coma not to want to watch cable news these days," says David Zurawik, media critic for the Baltimore *Sun*, "because what's happening is head-spinning."

A Day in the Life of Cable News

A day in the life of cable news begins around 6 a.m., more often than not with an off-the-wall tweet from the president. It's not unusual for him to be watching his favorite morning show *Fox & Friends* at the time, although early risers in the press corps are probably tuned to *Morning Joe* on MSNBC (which Trump used to like before he didn't).

Barring breaking news, a typical day in the White House is built around a few morning events and Press Secretary Sean Spicer's early afternoon press briefing. All three cable channels cover it live. If the president is not watching, he is recording it on his DVR to play back later.

RATINGS

Scoreboard: Thursday, May 18

*source: TV Newser (n millions)

Total Viewers
- **Primetime:** FNC: 2.488 | CNN: 1.485 | MSNBC: 2.499

	4p:	5p:	6p:	7p:	8p:	9p:	10p:	11p:
FOX NEWS channel	Cavuto: 1.720	Specialists: 1.839	Baier: 2.102	MacCallum: 1851	Carlson: 2.658	TheFive: 2.359	Hannity: 2.446	Carlson: 1.370
CNN	Tapper: 1.649	Blitzer: 1.463	Blitzer: 1.340	Burnett: 1.350	Cooper: 1.574	Cooper: 1.477	Lemon: 1.399	Lemon: 1.101
MSNBC	Wallace: 1.162	MTPDaily: 1.293	Greta: 1.115	Matthews: 1.844	Hayes: 2.054	Maddow: 2.940	O'Donnell: 2.496	Williams: 1.825

More Popular than General Hospital

The president has joked that Spicer's press conferences are more popular than *General Hospital*—"That guy gets great ratings," he told *The*

Washington Post—and he's not far off the mark. The soap opera draws an average of 2.6 million viewers a day. The combined audiences for Phil Cavuto, Jake Tapper and Nicolle Wallace, who comes on an hour later, are 4.5 million.

Once the briefing is over, the cable gabfest begins. On CNN, show hosts Brooke Baldwin, Jake Tapper, Wolf Blitzer, Erin Burnett, Anderson Cooper and Don Lemon lead viewers through eight hours of nonstop news, recycling key sound bites as many as 15 or 20 times and calling on various consultants and reporters for explication and commentary.

CNN calls this cast of characters "personalities" and lists 250 of them. Besides the show hosts, they include Dana Bash (chief political correspondent), John King (chief national correspondent), Gloria Borger (chief political analyst), Jeff Zeleny (senior White House correspondent) and 15 other correspondents who pop in and out of the shows as the stories dictate.

A Moderated Discussion

There are 54 other political analysts in the CNN stable. Twenty-eight are identified as liberal contributors, 26 are conservatives, and more than a dozen others are respected print journalists from other publications.

As the day progresses, panels of experts cycle in and out of the studio set more often than a hockey team changes lines. Frequent contributors who live in far-off cities have a green screen or skyline backdrop in their home so they can appear remotely, either alone or in a split screen with four or five others.

The show hosts are not traditional news anchors. They function more like agent provocateurs, calling up selected footage and bouncing questions off the experts. One advantage the cable news shows have over print is a library of campaign clips. When the president, for instance, announced that China was suddenly not manipulating its currency, CNN within minutes had four or five clips showing him denounce China for currency manipulation.

Without taking sides, or counting noses, CNN is bringing to the national conversation responsible voices from all parts of the spectrum. During the campaign, CNN's decision to pit Trump surrogates against Clinton surrogates often resulted in awkward standoffs between the two sides. What is happening now, however, is light years ahead of that. Most of the whiny truth benders are gone, and even Jeffrey Lord, Trump's apologist in chief, is wearing thin. "If Donald Trump took a dump on his desk, you would defend it," Anderson Cooper chided him the other night.

MSNBC Keeps Pace

MSNBC is creating its own on-air conversation pit with a lineup of NBC pros and a formidable Rolodex of print reporters, consultants, and inside the Beltway sources.

It wasn't long ago MSNBC was considered the left wing of cable news. Recent additions like Nicolle Wallace, the former communications director for George Bush, and Fox exile Greta Van Susteren have given it a more middle of the road feel. But its hosts—has anyone noticed they aren't called anchors anymore?—aren't shy about expressing their opinions.

Chris Matthews and Chuck Todd are veteran political reporters who relish mixing it up in the public arena. Chris Hayes is the newcomer who sometimes can be too smart for his own good. Lawrence O'Donnell is, well, Lawrence O'Donnell, a venerable opinion machine. And Brian Williams adds some gravitas batting cleanup in *The 11th Hour*, where he is serving out his sentence in journalistic rehab.

Somehow, it all works together because, for the first time in 17 years, MSNBC leads the cable ratings race. The big surprise in those ratings is Rachel Maddow, the arched brow liberal who is drawing Bill O'Reilly numbers (2.9 million viewers) in the primetime slot. Maddow delivers the news like she's backing up a truck to a loading dock, but her style is an odd mix of outrage and irony that leaves you feeling like it's okay to go to hell in a handbasket because whatever disaster comes next is going to be even more fun.

After suffering through a year of fake news, false innuendos, reality TV politics and outrageous tweets, I take pleasure these days in lying on the sofa with a remote clicker in hand, switching between the channels to watch first-rate journalists cover the burning dumpster that is The White House.

Odd Man Out

The odd man out in this conversation is the Fox News viewer. The network has been laboring all year under the shadow of sexual harassment charges. Its guiding light Roger Ailes was fired. Bill O'Reilly was forced out by an advertiser boycott, and its two most prominent female stars, Megyn Kelly and Van Susteren, left for greener pastures. That is a poor excuse, however, for Fox's willful failure to pursue the hottest story in Washington.

Last Friday, while MSNBC and CNN dug deeper into a breaking story on the Russia investigation, Fox was reporting on tornados in the Midwest, a Paul Ryan tax planning session, new field tactics to combat ISIS, and President Trump's ambitious foreign trip itinerary.

Sean Hannity pooh-poohed "sources from Mars" fueling the Russian meddling story. He had his own scoop to report, a conspiracy theory from the alt-right blogs that the Clinton campaign emails were actually leaked by a low-level Democratic staffer, Seth Rich. (Fox has since disavowed the report. Hannity so far has not.)

Make America Think Again

As hard as the Fox reporters work to get in a piece on the Russia investigation, the Fox anchors dismiss it. "If every story is Watergate, is any story Watergate?" Tucker Carlson scoffed. His message was clear. Move along, folks, nothing to see here. But viewers are not so easily fooled. Last week, the MSNBC audience was on the rise, and Fox fell to third place in the cable news ratings race.

Inside and outside the Beltway, concern over President Trump's fitness to lead the nation is growing, and two of the three cable channels are conducting a national conversation that delivers real news about real questions that will have a real effect on the nation. By habit or blind loyalty, viewers of Fox are denying themselves a chance to participate. They are sitting on the sidelines while America learns to think again and missing out on the opportunity to watch government at work.

— May 25, 2017

I Am a Rock,
I Am an Island,
I Am an Idiot

PRESIDENT TRUMP RETURNED SATURDAY to a red-faced nation after a nine-day trip to a world he doesn't understand.

"I think we hit a home run no matter where we were," he said. But he's the only one who thinks that. His sword dancing with the Saudi Crown Prince in Riyadh and bromance with Egyptian President Abdel Fattah el-Sisi ("Love your shoes, man") won't win any converts in the poor Arabian neighborhoods where terrorism breeds.

Leaving a note that could have been penned by a 10-year-old in the Book of Remember at the Yad Vashem holocaust memorial in Jerusalem doesn't instill confidence he can broker Israeli-Palestinian peace. "It's a great honor to be here with all of my friends. So amazing." And just ask Pope Francis how happy he was with their Vatican meeting, or look at the photos.

By the time the president got to Brussels for the NATO summit, Trump had pretty much exhausted his good graces. All he had to do was give a speech dedicating a memorial to the American, European and Canadian troops who died fighting in Afghanistan. The monument, a twisted piece of steel from the 9/11 attack on the World Trade Center, honors Article 5 of the NATO pact that holds an attack on one nation in the NATO alliance is an attack on all. For 70 years, it has been the glue holding NATO together, although it has only been invoked once—in defense of the United States.

Bungler in Chief

Everyone knows Trump wishes the other NATO nations would pay more for their own defense so it would not have been out of line for him to mention it in his speech. Other presidents going back to Ronald Reagan have taken the same position. But the gracious thing would have been to then pivot to America's commitment to Article 5, reassuring our allies that we are all in this together. Instead, he harangued the European leaders for taking in too many Middle East refugees and running up "massive" past due bills to the United States. That is not, by the way, how NATO works.

His ham-handed diplomacy bubbled over into a photo session where he got into a wrist-wrestling handshake with French President Emmanuel Macron. On a tour of the new NATO headquarters, he gratuitously chided the leaders for how much it cost. Then, in a separate meeting with our European Union partners, he called out Germany for its "bad, very bad" trade policies and threatened to stop importing German cars. He is apparently unaware that BMW, Mercedes-Benz and Volkswagen manufacture 850,000 autos a year here in assembly plants across the South and employ some 700,000 workers in America.

Beat It, Montenegro!

To top it off, in a move that became the symbol for his whole trip, he pushed his way past the prime minister of Montenegro to preen in front of the cameras at a photo-op of world leaders.

As if the NATO snub weren't enough, he flew on to a G-7 conference in Sicily where he all but fell asleep as the leaders of Canada, France, Germany, Japan, Italy and the United Kingdom made impassioned pleas for the U.S. to stay in the Paris climate accord. Pope Francis made a similar appeal in their private session and gave Trump his Encyclical on Climate Change as a parting gift.

Back on Terra Unfirma

Back home in America, Press Secretary Sean Spicer provided a jaw-dropping account of the journey. "It truly was an historic week for America and our people," he said. To underscore the point, he said "historic" five more times. "We've never seen before at this point in a presidency such sweeping reassurance of American interests and the inauguration of a foreign policy strategy designed to bring back the world from growing dangers and perpetual disasters brought on by years of failed leadership."

Trump's speech to the leaders of 50 Arab nations, Spicer added, "was a historic turning point that people will be talking about for many years to come." That's the one where he said *what*? Maybe in the White House they will, or in the president's Twitter account, which he took to as soon as he got back.

"Just returned from Europe. Trip was a great success for America. Hard work but big results!" he tweeted. Twenty minutes later, he was back to form tweeting about "fabricated lies" coming out of the White House press corps and the "poorly covered" Republican victory in a race for the Montana House seat.

The Blowback

While the president was tweeting, the blowback in Europe was just beginning. German Chancellor Angela Merkel told a campaign rally in Munich Trump's NATO appearance worried her. "The times when we could rely fully on others are to some extent over," she said. "I experienced that in the last few days. That is why we Europeans must really take our destiny into our own hands."

Macron said he too left Brussels and Sicily wary of dealing with Trump. "My handshake with him, it wasn't innocent," he told a French newspaper. "It was a moment of truth. One must show that you won't make small concessions, even symbolic ones, but also not over-publicize things."

In *Der Spiegel*, Germany's most popular newsweekly, Editor-in-Chief Klaus Brinkbaumer penned an editorial that quickly went viral. The opening paragraph was about as blunt as you can put it.

"Donald Trump has transformed the United States into a laughing-stock and he is a danger to the world. He must be removed from the White House before things get even worse."

Brinkbaumer detailed his case:

> *"Donald Trump is not fit to be president of the United States. He does not possess the requisite intellect and does not understand the significance of the office he holds nor the tasks associated with it. He doesn't read. He doesn't bother to peruse important files and intelligence reports and knows little about the issues that he has identified as his priorities. His decisions are capricious and they are delivered in the form of tyrannical decrees.*

> *"He is a man free of morals. As has been demonstrated hundreds of times, he is a liar, a racist and a cheat. I feel ashamed to use these words, as sharp and loud as they are. But if they apply to anyone, they apply to Trump. And one of the media's tasks is to continue telling things as they are. Trump has to be removed from the White House. Quickly. He is a danger to the world."*

Left and Right Agree

It's not hard to find pundits in America who think Trump's first foreign adventure was an embarrassment to himself and America. "Trump thinks the way to represent America is with a caricature of strength, without understanding it comes across as weakness and boorishness. Even with the weightiest job in the world, he can't seem to mature beyond the schoolyard bully," Maureen Dowd wrote in her Sunday *New York Times* column.

Charlie Sykes, the conservative radio commentator from Wisconsin, characterized the president's approach as "thin-skinned nastiness masquerading as confidence." And CNN's Chris Cillizza called Spicer's description of the European meetings as "a trip to an alternate universe."

How's It Playing in Trump Country?

There are people who say it doesn't matter what Europe thinks as long as the president can hold onto his base, that vast swath of Middle America hankering to drain the swamp in Washington. So far, the investigation into Russian tampering with the election hasn't moved the meter in their opinions. The detrimental effects of repealing Obamacare, cutting taxes for the wealthy, or scaling back social programs they rely on doesn't seem to faze them.

But when the president goes abroad and embarrasses America on the world stage, he's tampering with our American pride. That pride is born of the feeling we're pretty good people. We work hard, we play hard, but we have generous hearts. We treat other people with respect, and we expect them to treat us with respect. We're happy the German automakers are building factories here. We're ready to stand shoulder to shoulder with our NATO allies to defend freedom. We want to do our part to make the world a safer, healthier place.

That's what making America great means. But to Trump it's just a slogan. Now he's got a new slogan. "America First." But everything he did in Europe said, "Me First." He wasn't representing America. His trip was all about me, me, me.

The America I know makes friends out of enemies, not enemies out of friends. We do that by gaining their respect. And nobody respects an idiot. So President Trump really ought to cut it out and start showing the world *why* America is great.

— May 31, 2017

Not the Only
Show in Town

Lost in President Trump's Twitter-trending tiff with Psycho Joe Scarborough and Crazy Mika Brzezinski were reports this week that a new Ford Focus plant in Mexico, which President Trump decried on the campaign trail, will now relocate to China.

This follows on the heels of the president's first foray to Europe where German Chancellor Angela Merkel declared that Europe can no longer "fully rely" on its United States ally, and before Secretary of Commerce Wilbur Ross's video address to a European business conference was abruptly cut off mid-speech, to cheers and applause from attendees.

The Trump administration's plan to put America First on the world stage is right on schedule. The only problem is nobody is lining up behind us. According to a recent survey by the Pew Research Center of people across 37 nations, confidence in America's leadership has dropped from 64% to 22% since Trump took office, in no small part due to our president's tweets.

We are well past that day in 2015 when Trump announced his candidacy for president, and the *Huffington Post* said it would cover his campaign on the Entertainment Page. He ran and won. But with every passing day, he demonstrates he is woefully (and maybe willfully) ignorant of the responsibilities of the office. He likes the pageantry of signing his name to executive orders, the adulation he can command at a cabinet meeting, and those high-level photo-ops with foreign leaders.

But when he wakes up every morning, what is he thinking? What are Joe and Mika saying about me on *Morning Joe*? Did China's Xi Jinping like the chocolate cake at Mar-a-Lago? How did Arnold Schwarzenegger do last night in the ratings?

Modern Day Presidential

He calls his Twitter feed "modern day presidential" because it allows him to speak directly to the American people. But this unfiltered, self-aggrandizing version of his performance has earned him 67 "Pants on Fire!" ratings from *PolitiFact*. The president's Twitter account has become easy pickings for reporters looking to take a poke at the president. What began with fact checks has evolved into news analysis stories describing Trump's behavior as "surprising," "startling," "head-scratching" and "beneath the dignity of the office."

Although no one wants to flat out call him "crazy"—a word Trump has used 100 times in his Twitter account to describe his enemies—it's become increasingly clear he is off his rocker.

House Speaker Paul Ryan says Trump's Twitter feed compromises his ability to get things done in Washington. "What we're trying to do around here is improve the civility and tone of the debate, and this obviously does not do that." But that's like telling a boy brandishing a gun in class to mind his manners.

Tweet Away!

I say tweet away, Mr. President. Plop your feet up on the desk in front of your widescreen TV and f-bomb every dumb shit who crosses your path. Just do it in a locked room where the Secret Service can feed you executive orders through a slot in the door and run them by the sanity police before they are released.

Sticks and stones (and presidential actions) can break my bones, but tweets can never hurt me. So let the turtle out on your opinions, @realDonaldTrump. Maybe we can get *The New York Times* to publish a column of them every day on the Op-Ed page in a box called *Fake News!*

— July 5, 2017

The Lonely Life
of I Alone

Last week marked the first anniversary of Donald Trump's "I Alone" speech to the Republican convention. In one of the great panders of politics—and politics is full of them—the Republican nominee recounted all that ails America, and he had a solution for all of them.

"Nobody knows the system better than me," he said, "which is why I alone can fix it."

So six months into his term, how's he doing?

"The W.H. is functioning perfectly," he tweeted. "I have very little time for watching TV." Then he trashed his attorney general, replaced Sean

119

Spicer with Anthony Scaramucci as his communications director...and changed the channel.

A Pugnacious Sort

We have all had to lower our standards for leadership in this administration, but is it too much to ask I Alone not to turn every policy debate into a referendum on his own fragile ego?

Whether he is feuding with the media over his inauguration crowd or berating federal judges for halting his Muslim travel ban, his determination to show he can say or do anything he damn well pleases as president isn't just delusional, it's a cancerous obsession.

"This is a president who fights fire with fire and certainly will not be allowed to be bullied by liberal media and the liberal elites within the media or Hollywood or anywhere else," Sarah Huckabee Sanders, his new press secretary, said at the height of his kerfuffle with *Morning Joe* and Mika.

But you don't have to be liberal to earn his ire. He has harsh words for any Republican who stands in the way of a health care bill. His Twitter account drips with disdain for CNN, the failing *New York Times*, and the Amazon *Washington Post*. And don't get him started on the Mueller investigation, that slow-rolling tar ball coming up Pennsylvania Avenue and scooping up everything in its path, including his son.

Pomp and Circumstance

When he is not on Twitter or glued to the TV, I Alone likes the pomp and circumstance of signing executive orders. He likes it so much he sometimes signs things that aren't orders at all, just stuff he'd like to see happen. Most of the real bills he signs are regulatory rollbacks or routine housekeeping. But every signing is another occasion to remind people he is making America great again—like the country can be saved by a slogan—by renaming a VA health center in rural Pennsylvania.

To focus I Alone on the issues, his staff sets up elaborate rollout plans for Infrastructure Week, and Tech Week, and Made-in-America Week. I Alone sleepwalks through them like he's touring a county fair exhibit. His real comfort zone is the campaign rally where, surrounded by fawning fans, he can flog old enemies (Crooked Hillary) and perceived new ones (disloyal Republicans), or ramble on about whatever pops into his head.

Drain the Swamp

A surefire applause line at those rallies is his promise to drain the swamp in Washington. But the swamp only seems to have gotten murkier since he took office. His cabinet is stuffed with millionaires and billionaires, three of whom—Scott Pruitt at the EPA, Rick Perry in Energy and Betsy DeVos at Education—are running departments they think shouldn't exist.

Goldman Sachs, the Wall Street firm his campaign commercials claimed "robbed our working class" and "stripped our country of its wealth," has contributed four partners to his White House economic team. Gary Cohn, Steven Mnuchin, Jim Donovan and Dina Powell. One ex-partner, Anthony Scaramucci, is his director of communications.

They occupy a White House teeming with people who don't much like each other (not unlike *The Apprentice*). There's the Bannon faction and the Kushner faction, the national security advisers, an ever-changing lineup of press spokesmen, and now, the lawyer faction. Which one is on top depends on who has the president's ear on any particular day.

On the day-to-day level of keeping the government wheels turning, meanwhile, other federal departments labor under a dearth of leadership. In his first week in office, I Alone fired all of our ambassadors overseas and all 93 U.S. Attorneys in the Justice Department. Six months into his administration, only a handful of ambassadors have been confirmed as replacements, and 91 of the 93 U.S. Attorney posts remain vacant.

Secretary of State Rex Tillerson is running pillar to post trying to put out fires in Syria, Yemen, North Korea, Ukraine and Qatar—I Alone started that one—without ambassadors in South Korea, Saudi Arabia, India, Germany, France, Britain and Russia. Fifty-seven other key diplomatic posts, including six undersecretary jobs, don't even have nominees waiting for confirmation.

Of the 570 executive branch positions that require Senate approval, only 50 have been confirmed—compared with 200 at this point in the administrations of Barack Obama, George W. Bush and Bill Clinton. And there are no names in the hopper for 375 others. Tillerson, meanwhile, is so frustrated by his role in the administration he is ready to resign by the end of the year.

The White House justifiably complains Senate Democrats are slow-walking nominees through the confirmation process. (They are.) But the line of people awaiting approval is short because I Alone insists on weeding out candidates who opposed him in the primaries, and many qualified career officials want no part of an administration that won't listen to them.

On the World Stage

In his two trips abroad, the president has cultivated his image as a buffoon, mingling uncomfortably with other world leaders and managing to say all the wrong things, in all the wrong places.

In six short months, the world's confidence in American leadership has dropped from 64% to 22%, according to a Pew Research survey. In interviews with 40,000 people in 37 countries, 75% of respondents describe our president as "arrogant," 65% as "intolerant" and 62% as "dangerous."

Domestic Tranquility?

His standing at home is not much better. His approval rating in the latest ABC/Washington Post poll has dropped from 40% to 36%, the worst performance by a new president in 70 years.

Can it get worse? Probably not. Another poll taken at the same time reports that 32% of Trump supporters don't believe his son Donald Jr. met with a Russian lawyer (even after the campaign confirmed it). So there's a floor to the intelligence of voters, and I Alone is bobbing just above it.

I Alone Can't Fix It

For all his vaunted skills as a dealmaker, Trump can't rub two senators together to get a health care bill over the finish line. (Although it might help if he understood it.) As the Senate voted to take up the health care debate, I Alone retreated into his tweets and rallies. The role of statesman thus fell to Sen. John McCain, returning to the Senate floor after surgery for a brain tumor.

"We're getting nothing done. Our health care insurance system is a mess. We all know it, those who support Obamacare and those who oppose it. Something has to be done," McCain said. "We Republicans have looked for a way to end it and replace it with something else without paying a terrible political price. We haven't found it yet, and I'm not sure we will. All we've managed to do is make more popular a policy that wasn't very popular when we started trying to get rid of it.

"Let's hold hearings, try to report a bill out of committee with contributions from both sides. Then bring it to the floor for amendment and debate. Let's see if we can pass something that will be imperfect, full of compromises, and not very pleasing to implacable partisans on either side, but that might provide workable solutions to the problems Americans are struggling with today," he added.

For months I Alone has been telling us he's waiting pen in hand in the Oval Office to sign a health care bill. Sending him one that enjoys bipartisan support, reflects the input of doctors, hospitals and patient care advocates, and protects the hard-won benefits of Obamacare would go a long way to restoring our faith in government.

You might even call it a win. And there's nothing I Alone likes more than a win, as long as he gets credit for it.

— July 26, 2017

Watch Out for That Flying Bag of Dope

NOW THAT WE'VE PUT HEALTH CARE TO BED—for the time being—we can get back to a more pressing issue facing America. How to build that Mexican Wall.

When last I checked in, President Trump had just sacrificed the careers of 15,000 transgender soldiers to get House Republicans to put a $1.6 billion allocation for the wall in the 2018 federal budget. That will get it started, but it's hardly enough to put a dent in the landscape. The latest Homeland Security estimate is $21.6 billion, or five times what it will cost to send a space mission to Mars.

First Things First

One of his first things Trump did when he came into office was commission eight prototype wall panels to be built on a demonstration site outside San Diego this fall. Each panel must be 30 feet high and run at least six feet underground to prevent tunneling. Over 460 bidders submitted proposals, not all serious.

There were so many good ideas for a solar-powered wall in that Trump told a rally in Iowa we ought to do that because it would really save us a lot on electricity. "Think about it. The higher it goes, the more valuable it is," he said.

Three weeks ago, on board Air Force One on his way to Paris for Bastille Day, the president started ruminating with Maggie Haberman of *The New York Times* about another good idea he had for the wall.

"One of the things with the wall is you need transparency. You have to be able to see through it. In other words, if you can't see through that wall, it won't work. You have to have openings because you have to see what's on the other side of the wall."

"And I'll give you an example. As horrible as it sounds, when they throw the large sacks of drugs over, and if you have people on the other side of the wall, you don't see them—they hit you on the head with 60 pounds of stuff. It's over. As crazy as that sounds, you need transparency through that wall. But we have some incredible designs."

Strongman Wanted

Let me repeat that: "When they throw the large sacks of drugs over...they hit you on the head with 60 pounds of stuff."

Eric Zorn of the *Chicago Tribune* wasn't the only reporter who did a double take when he read that. "The idea of ultra-strong smugglers blindly flinging large bags of illegal drugs over the border and conking people on the head. That's nutty. Daft. Blithely detached from reality in a way that would be deeply disturbing in a village trustee, let alone the president of the United States."

A Record Toss

My favorite reaction came from Philip Bump of *The Washington Post*, who set about finding the world record for throwing a 60-pound sack of anything. He discovered the American Strongman Contest has a keg tossing event that Hafthor Bjornsson, who plays The Mountain on *Game of Thrones*, won last year with a toss of 24 feet, 6 inches. The keg weighed only 33 pounds, but observers said the keg actually went some 28 feet up in the air. Unfortunately, the minimum wall spec is two feet higher.

In Scotland, Bjornsson also holds the world record in The Highland Games for an event called "weight over bar." That requires throwing a 56-pound weight from a standing position, and Bjornsson set the record with a toss of 19 feet, 7 inches. Paul Mouser, the lead sponsor of the strongman competition, says he doubts Bjornsson could ever get a 60-pound sack over the wall. For that, you would need a catapult, he says.

But why do we need a wall anyway? Our president has done such a good job of scaring the bejesus out of immigrants nobody wants to come to America anymore.

Who wants to come to a place where you can get hit on the head by a 60-pound bag of dope just walking down the street?

— July 31, 2017

Russia

Donald J. Trump ✔
@realDonaldTrump

Russia has never tried to use leverage over me. I HAVE NOTHING TO DO WITH RUSSIA - NO DEALS, NO LOANS, NO NOTHING!

RETWEETS   LIKES
23,664   86,348   

6:31 AM - 11 Jan 2017

Trump Did It!

SO LET'S STATE THE OBVIOUS. Gen. Michael Flynn called the Russian Embassy to discuss lifting President Obama's sanctions for election meddling because then President-elect Trump asked him to.

Trump may not have been sitting over Flynn's shoulder when he made the call, but it's becoming increasingly clear that Flynn didn't go rogue. He was Trump's national security adviser carrying out Trump's desire for a détente with Russia the only way he knew how, with stealth and cunning. Better relations with Russia was a centerpiece of Trump's campaign, and Flynn made it his priority.

Even though President Obama had warned Trump that Flynn was a loose cannon, Trump knew Flynn had many back-channel connections in Russia. His appearance next to Vladimir Putin at a Russian RT banquet in 2015 was no secret, so it was no surprise when, on Dec. 19, Flynn called Sergey Kislyak, the Russian ambassador to the U.S., to express his condolences for the terrorist assassination of the Russian ambassador to Turkey. Nor was it a surprise on Christmas Eve, when he exchanged Christmas greetings with Kislyak via text.

But these seemingly innocent contacts took an ominous turn on Dec. 29 when President Obama imposed sanctions on Russia and expelled 35 Russian diplomats for Russia's hacking of the U.S. elections. This time, Flynn called Kislyak at the embassy and U.S. intelligence agents were listening in. It is a long-standing tradition that incoming presidents are expected not to interfere with the actions of outgoing ones, but Trump has never been known for observing niceties. Flynn asked Kislyak not to respond until Trump was in office, and sure enough the next day, President Putin said he was standing down. "Although we have the right to retaliate," he said, "we will not resort to irresponsible 'kitchen' diplomacy but will plan our further steps to restore Russian-US relations based on the policies of the Trump Administration."

"Great move on delay (by V. Putin)," Trump tweeted. "I always knew he was very smart!"

The Investigation That Wouldn't Go Away

Over the next 10 days, Trump Tower was a beehive of activity. Between interviewing potential cabinet members, greeting celebrities and planning his first 100 days, President Trump sat down on Friday, Jan. 6 for a briefing on the Russian hack from U.S. intelligence agencies. He was impatient to get it over with, and skeptical that he would learn much.

But there was more substance in the briefing than he imagined, and something he didn't foresee: a dossier from a British intelligence agent that alleged various contacts between Trump associates and Russian operatives and a salacious charge, not substantiated, that Trump had been videotaped in a hotel room with Russian prostitutes on a visit to Moscow.

After the briefing, Trump unleashed a Saturday morning tweet storm pooh-poohing the notion his campaign was in cahoots with the Russians. "Having a good relationship with Russia is a good thing, not a bad thing. Only 'stupid' people, or fools, would think that it is bad!" he said.

"We have enough problems around the world without yet another one. When I am President, Russia will respect us far more than they do now," he added, "and both countries will, perhaps, work together to solve some of the many great and pressing problems and issues of the WORLD!"

Three days later, *Buzzfeed* published the entire dossier. Trump's Twitter feed exploded.

Tweet 1: *FAKE NEWS—A TOTAL POLITICAL WITCH HUNT!*

Tweet 2: *Russia just said the unverified report paid for by political opponents is "A COMPLETE AND TOTAL FABRICATION, UTTER NONSENSE." Very unfair!*

Tweet 3: *Russia has never tried to use leverage over me. I HAVE NOTHING TO DO WITH RUSSIA—NO DEALS, NO LOANS, NO NOTHING!*

An Asset, Not a Liability

The *Buzzfeed* document dump came on the same day Trump was holding his first post-election press conference in Manhattan. Reluctantly, Trump conceded, "As far as hacking, I think it was Russia. But I think we also get hacked by other countries and other people."

"If Putin likes Donald Trump, guess what, folks, that's considered an asset not a liability," he added. "Now I don't know that I'm going to get along with Premier Putin. I hope I do. But if I don't, do you honestly believe that Hillary will be tougher on Putin than me?"

The next day, David Ignatius reported for the first time in *The Washington Post* that Gen. Flynn not only called Kislyak to discuss the sanctions on the day Obama announced them, but they spoke several times.

"After this past week of salacious leaks about foreign espionage plots and indignant denials, people must be wondering if something is rotten in the state of our democracy," Ignatius wrote. "How can we dispel the dark rumors that, as Hamlet says, shake our disposition?"

One person who moved immediately to dispel the dark rumors was Sen. Richard Burr (R-N.C.). He announced his Senate Intelligence Committee would "expeditiously" conduct an investigation into Russian hacking as well as "any intelligence regarding links between Russia and individuals associated with political campaigns."

Press Secretary Sean Spicer pushed back the next day. The only phone call Flynn made on Dec. 29 was "centered on the logistics" of a post-inauguration congratulatory call between Trump and Putin. "That was it, plain and simple."

On the Sunday talk shows, Vice President Pence told Fox News that Flynn assured him "the conversations that took place at that time were not in any way related to the new U.S. sanctions against Russia or the expulsion of diplomats." And White House Chief of Staff Reince Priebus told *Meet the Press* the subject of sanctions never came up in his conversations with Flynn.

Silence at the Core

Notably silent in the denials was Trump himself. How could he not know what Flynn was talking about with Kislyak when he was simultaneously tweeting about it? And Flynn wasn't the only Trump associate talking with the Russians. Trump's attorney general, Jeff Sessions, spoke with Kislyak at the Republican convention. Former campaign manager Paul Manafort, foreign policy adviser Carter Page, longtime confidant Roger Stone and Trump personal attorney Michael Cohen were also in conversations with Russian operatives. His sons Donald Jr. and Eric were in and out of Russia doing business deals.

On Twitter, the president vociferously insists he has no loans or deals in Russia *currently*. But it's fair to say his confidence in his ability to deal with Vladimir Putin stems from his past experience working with Russian partners.

A Riddle, Wrapped in a Mystery, Inside an Enigma

To do business in Russia, you have to think like a Russian, approaching every problem like you are peeling away the skin of an onion. You have to recognize there is a web of connections between business and government. Someone you meet in one capacity, a tour guide, for instance, might be helpful in another. He might have an uncle who works for a company owned by an oligarch who was in the KGB with a state official who oversees Moscow land development. (Or he might just be a Russian agent.) A business deal doesn't come together in Russia without a string of hangers-on attached, and somehow it always runs through a government channel.

As Winston Churchill famously observed, Russia is a riddle, wrapped in a mystery, inside an enigma. Less famous, but equally important, was his addendum: "The key is Russian national interest."

Leaving the president out of the equation for the moment, the Trump Organization is rife with Russia-related deals: golf courses that Eric Trump says were financed by Russian banks, scores of luxury apartments purchased by Russian oligarchs, hotels, resorts and other business partnerships where Trump has sold his name to a consortium of foreign investors.

In the enigma that is Trump, the only national interest is Trump's interest. Although elected to represent the American interest, his first instinct is to insert himself into every deal. But first, potential partners must pass through a close circle of friends and family. As his national security adviser, Flynn was as close as you can get to Trump without being family. He was empowered to make promises on behalf of the president. If something went awry, Trump would have a shield of deniability—even if it was only a bald-faced lie on Twitter.

"What Report Was That?"

On Feb. 9, *The Washington Post* published another front-page story reaffirming that Flynn discussed U.S. sanctions with the Russian ambassador. Nine intelligence sources confirmed the discussion. Two of them said Flynn explicitly urged Kislyak not to overreact because the matter could be revisited after Trump was sworn in.

On his way to a weekend in Mar-a-Logo, Trump played dumb. "What report is that? I haven't seen that. I'll look into that," he said. But Deputy Attorney General Sally Yates says she gave details of Flynn's conversation to the White House counsel in two meetings on Jan. 26 and 27.

Four days after the *Post* story, Flynn was asked to resign. The reason offered by Sean Spicer was that he lied to the vice president. Even after his departure, however, Trump insisted that Flynn was an honorable man who did nothing wrong. "He was doing his job. He was calling countries. I didn't direct him, but I would have directed him if he didn't do it," he explained.

Blackmail or Loyalty

There has been much consternation in the press over the 18-day gap between when Yates reported Flynn's misconduct and his firing. No sooner was Yates out the door—dramatically fired over her refusal to implement the Muslim travel ban—than Flynn was sitting in on an hourlong phone conversation between Trump and President Putin.

"The underlying conduct of Gen. Flynn was problematic in itself," Yates told Congress, but his willingness to lie about the nature of his call to the Russian ambassador meant he could "essentially be blackmailed by the Russians."

The president called her testimony old hat. How could the Russians blackmail Flynn for doing what the president asked him to do? His offense, remember, wasn't lying to the president. It was lying to the vice president. And nobody tells him anything.

— May 11, 2017

The Russian Connection

I'M GOING TO GO OUT ON A LIMB HERE and surmise that the connection between the Trump campaign and the Russians was Donald Trump himself.

He had the means, the motive and the opportunity to contact the Russians in the last election—and he's the only one in the campaign with the chutzpah to do it.

Hollow Denials

I've heard his denials. We all have, so many times, in so many ways, that the latest CNN poll shows 73% of Americans don't believe anything they hear coming out of his mouth. The president has squandered his right to be taken at his word on this subject, so the door is now open for speculation on the various paths that collusion between the campaign and Russia might have taken.

Let the House and Senate Intelligence committees flail around in the smoke of odd coincidences looking for fire. What if it's not all that complicated?

Turn the Questions Around

What if Gen. Michael Flynn, Trump's first national security adviser, called Russian Ambassador Sergey Kislyak on the same day President Obama imposed sanctions because Trump told him to?

What if Trump and Aras Agalarov, the Russian oligarch he partnered with to bring the Miss Universe pageant to Moscow, arranged the Trump Tower meeting with his son Donald Jr. to pass along dirt on Hillary Clinton? (And Don Jr. blew the cover by inviting Jared Kushner and Paul Manafort.)

What if Trump hired his best friend Roger Stone's old business partner Paul Manafort as his campaign manager precisely because Manafort gave him a conduit to the Russians with plausible deniability?

What if Vladimir Putin wasn't trying to get to Trump through various intermediaries? What if Trump was trying to get to Putin to demonstrate his willingness to reset American-Russian relations—if only he could get elected?

Courting Putin

Trump had been courting Putin even before the 2013 pageant opened. "Do you think Putin will be going to The Miss Universe Pageant in November in Moscow—if so, will he become my new best friend," he tweeted when the pageant was announced.

Putin did not attend, but he did send a "beautiful present, with a beautiful note," Trump told the Conservative Political Action Conference in March 2014. "I spoke to all of his people. And, you know, you look at what he's doing to President Obama. He's, like, toying with him."

In May that same year, Trump again told the National Press Club, "I spoke directly and indirectly with President Putin, who could not have been nicer." And in November 2015 he said, "I got to know him very well because we were both on '60 Minutes.'" (Not to be contrarian, but *Time* magazine noted they were interviewed separately in New York and Moscow for the show.)

After gaining the Republican nomination in July 2016—five days after WikiLeaks released 44,000 emails Russian hackers stole from the Democratic National Committee—Trump changed his tune.

"I never met Putin. I don't know who Putin is," he told a press conference. But he couldn't let it go at that. "Russia, if you're listening, I hope you're able to find the 30,000 emails that are missing," he added.

Multitasking

It boggles the mind to think that Trump could go 16 months on the presidential campaign trail without talking to his Russian friends about business. He had Trump International Hotel deals brewing in Moscow, Istanbul, Manila and Baku (Azerbaijan), all of which involved foreign investors. He wasn't going to just let those deals swing in the wind while he indulged his presidential passion.

Talking Points Memo recently interviewed Felix Sater, Trump's business partner in the Trump Soho complex. Sater once had offices in Trump Tower, and he says he was actively working with Trump on a hotel deal in Moscow as late as December 2015—six months after Trump announced his candidacy. Prior to that, Trump had a signed agreement with Agalarov to develop another Moscow hotel property that fell through.

Listening In

I've often wondered about President Trump's tweet last March claiming President Obama "had my wires tapped" in Trump Tower. Officials in the intelligence community have explained, in some detail, the many safeguards that are in place to prevent this. And yet Trump has convinced himself it must have happened.

How else could the FBI be sure he was colluding with the Russians unless they tapped his phones? They *must* have been listening in on his private conversations.

Too Confused to Collude

Jared Kushner was probably more right than wrong when he told congressional interns last week the Trump campaign was too confused to collude with the Russians. "They thought we colluded, but we couldn't even collude with our local offices."

If the campaign was disorganized, no one was more disorganized than the candidate. He was all over the map in his speeches, his tweets, his facts, and, especially, his memory of what he just said. Who's to say Trump didn't call one of his Russian friends—one of Putin's people, as he calls them—to talk at length about his travails running for president against Crooked Hillary, then forgot about it the next day?

'I Love It'

The June 9 meeting between Donald Trump Jr. and the Russian attorney is a guide to Trump's selective memory.

Rob Goldstone, a British publicist working for Agalarov, got the ball rolling with a June 3 email to Don Jr. promising he had dirt from the highest levels of the Kremlin on Hillary Clinton misdeeds.

"I'm sending this to you," Goldstone wrote, "or should I just have my guy call Rhona?" Rhona Graff is Trump's personal secretary of 30 years and the person to call if you want to speak with the boss.

"I love it," Don Jr. replied.

On June 7, Goldstone followed up with an email confirming a meeting in Trump Tower. That was the same day Trump won the California and New Jersey primaries. "I am going to give a major speech on probably Monday of next week, and we're going to be discussing all of the things that have taken place with the Clintons," Trump told a rally the next day.

"I think you're going to find it very informative and very, very interesting. I wonder if the press will want to attend. Who knows?"

The Trump Tower meeting lasted only 20-30 minutes, according to Don Jr., Kushner and Manafort. Despite the bombshell potential, none of them bothered to tell the president about it before or after the meeting—or so they say.

A Selective Memory

While Trump was off at the G-20 summit in Europe, *The New York Times* contacted Don Jr. on July 7 for his reaction to a story it was preparing about the meeting. That was the summit where President Trump met with Putin, but Secretary of State Rex Tillerson, the only American who accompanied him, said they discussed election meddling, Syria and a joint cyberterrorism initiative. But there was a second conversation that night between Trump and Putin at the G-20 dinner that was witnessed only by Putin's interpreter.

The next day, flying home on Air Force One, the president dictated a response from Don Jr. that ran along with the story on July 8. The timeline suggests Trump may have heard of the *Times* inquiry between meetings with Putin, and he used the second conversation to alert Putin, or ask his advice on how to handle it.

His dictated response turned out to be so misleading that Don Jr.'s lawyers twice had to correct it. Finally, the lawyers released all the emails leading up to the meeting (after being told *The New York Times* already had them). Interviewed by Reuters on July 12, Trump said he only learned of the meeting "a couple days ago." That would be after he doctored his son's response.

A Tangled Web

Robert Mueller's investigation is working its way up the evidence chain, following foreign intercepts and financial records to uncover how Russia coordinated its effort to interfere with the 2016 election with the Trump campaign. But if you pull the string on all Trump's lies, it's just as likely Trump was trying to play the Russians through the same intermediaries.

"I never get too attached to one deal or one approach," he wrote in *The Art of the Deal*, "I keep a lot of balls in the air, because most deals fall out, no matter how promising they seem at first. In addition, once I've made a deal, I always come up with at least a half dozen approaches to making it work, because anything can happen, even to the best-laid plans."

This reminds me of a childhood verse my mother impressed on me in my youth: "Oh what a tangled web we weave when first we practice to deceive."

What a tangled web, indeed.

— October 8, 2017

In the Room
Where It Happened

WHILE THE BOOK WORLD TITTERS over Mary Trump's takedown of Uncle Donald in *Too Much and Never Enough*, I've been spending my time in John Bolton's memoir of his tenure as President Trump's national security adviser.

For 14 months, Bolton puts us *In the Room Where It Happened* when Trump made critical decisions about North Korea, Russia, Syria, Turkey, NATO, China, Cuba, Venezuela, Afghanistan, Iran and Ukraine. (For 700 pages. Bolton was a prodigious notetaker.) And he came away with his head spinning. President Trump was in way over his head.

"He second-guessed people's motives, saw conspiracies behind rocks, and remained stunningly uninformed on how to run the White House, let along the huge federal government. He believed he could run the Executive Branch and establish national security policies on instinct, relying on personal relationships with foreign leaders, and with made-for-television showmanship always top of mind."

First Contact

Bolton was Trump's third national security adviser in two years, following on the heels of H.R. McMaster. Trump knew Bolton from his days as a Fox News commentator. A familiar figure in Washington's corridors of power, Bolton interviewed for a variety of foreign policy posts during the transition but was passed over for being too hawkish.

He bluntly warned Trump—as did President Obama—that North Korea's nuclear aspirations loomed as his biggest problem. And the time for military intervention was running out. Bolton outlined for Trump his alternatives: 1) regime change, 2) some tricky negotiations aimed at a reunification of the Korean Peninsula, or 3) a preemptive strike on North Korea's nuclear facilities coupled with a surprise attack on North Korea's artillery along the DMZ.

Bolton watched from the sidelines as Trump stumbled into a Twitter war with Kim Jong Un, promising "Fire and Fury" in one tweet, calling him "Rocketman" in a UN speech, and, like a teenager, taunting Kim on Twitter that my nuclear button is bigger than your nuclear button. When McMaster tired of Trump's fickle pronouncements, Gen. John Kelly, Trump's chief of staff, recommended Bolton to succeed him in March 2018.

A Chaotic Process

Bolton's first taste of foreign service came in the administration of President George H.W. Bush, whose National Security Council ran like clockwork. Every night, the staff would sift through intelligence reports from 17 difference agencies and put the most pressing into a President's Daily Brief (PDB) that could run as long as 60 pages. (President Obama read it every morning.)

President Bush's daily briefing started promptly at 8 a.m. The first 15 minutes consisted of the CIA director presenting the highlights, followed by a 30-minute discussion of the most pressing issues, then another 45-minute private meeting between Bush and his national security adviser Brent Scowcroft.

President Trump, by contrast, likes to start his day with "Executive Time" in the residence until about 11 a.m. That gives him time to call friends and watch TV. He cut back his briefings to twice a week, and if you think he reads the PDB, you're dreaming. He never reads it, or much of anything, including emails from top advisers.

McMaster tried to get around Trump's aversion to reading by putting the most significant topics into a PowerPoint. (Trump particularly liked seeing satellite spy cam footage.) Bolton tried switching out the presenter until he found a woman whose deference seemed to please Trump. But it really didn't matter because, in most meetings, Trump liked to do all the talking.

"He spent a disproportionate share of his time watching his administration being covered in the press," Bolton writes, and it didn't make Bolton's job any easier. "It was like making and executing policy inside a pinball machine."

First Crisis

Bolton's first day at the White House followed a weekend when Syria's Bashar Assad used chemical weapons on civilians in Douma. The president responded immediately—with a tweet. "Many dead, including women and children, in mindless CHEMICAL attack in Syria...Russia and Iran are responsible for backing Animal Assad. Big price to pay."

Britain and France wanted to join the U.S. in a joint retaliatory attack, with targets ranging from Syria's five major military airfields (high risk) to the factories and labs where the U.S. suspected the weapons were being made (low risk). The heads of the intelligence agencies, key cabinet members and the president gathered for a meeting of the National Security Council Principals Committee.

"We had to consider not just the immediate response but what Syria, Russia and Iran might do next," Bolton writes, and Trump's presence wasn't helpful. "He wasn't clear about what he wanted, jumping randomly from one question to another, and generally frustrating efforts to have a coherent discussion about the consequences."

Eventually, they agreed to attack Syria's chemical plants. On the day set for the attack, Bolton got a call from Kelly. Trump wanted to go over the strike package again.

"I don't love the targets," Trump said. "It could be criticized as doing nothing." What if he just tweeted out that we planned to attack, then didn't? Bolton couldn't believe that after working out all the logistics for times, munitions, launch bases, and targets among three nations, Trump wanted to change the plan.

"We're knocking out nothing," the president went on. Then he asked why Germany wasn't contributing to the strike, and why Germany was building an oil pipeline to Russia. In the end, he relented.

"We'll take that as a go order," Kelly said, closing off any further detours. The attack went off without a hitch. When Bolton told Kelly the whole process seemed fruitless, Kelly shrugged, "You're going to be very frustrated in this job."

The Singapore Summit

Inspired by North Korea's first appearance at the 2018 Olympics in February, Kim's sister told her South Koreans hosts they'd welcome a chance to speak directly to the American president. Trump quickly accepted. "I'm a talker, I like to talk," he boasted.

The summit was set for June 12 in Singapore. One of Bolton's first jobs was to make it happen. His next job was to make it mean something. Secretary of State Mike Pompeo was dispatched to Pyongyang to make the arrangements. The North Koreans refused to negotiate with Bolton.

The official position of the United States was that the president would not attend unless the summit led to an agreement for "complete, verifiable and irreversible de-nuclearization" of the Korean Peninsula. The North Koreans countered they would work toward de-nuclearization—without the "complete, verifiable and irreversible" part—in exchange for the U.S. lifting sanctions.

Pompeo couldn't bridge the gap so, on May 24, Trump sent Kim a letter saying that the summit was off. The next day, it was back on. A White House reporter called it "head-snapping diplomacy." When Bolton asked Trump why he changed his mind, he said he didn't want to lose the momentum. "This is a big win here. If we make a deal, it will be one of the greatest deals in history."

Pompeo was making no headway on a formal agreement, so one morning, a frustrated Trump decided he would handle it himself. "Get the leader of the delegation on the phone," he ordered. Soon enough Trump found himself speaking to a low-level foreign service officer in Korea. "I'm the one to sell this deal," he told the startled aide, "You shouldn't negotiate de-nuclearization, and you should tell them that."

Trump wavered back and forth on whether to go to the summit, but finally made a decision. "I want to go. It will be great theater." Two days later, a North Korean diplomat delivered a "beautiful letter" from Kim to Trump at the White House. The president read it and passed it on to Bolton. "The letter was pure puffery, written probably by some clerk in North Korea's agitprop bureau, but Trump loved it," Bolton writes. The Singapore Summit was on.

Trump and Kim met for an hour. When he saw video of North Korea's recent ballistic missile tests, Trump told Kim he saw a beautiful coastline that would make a great tourist resort. "Think of it from a real estate perspective," he said. "You could have the best hotels in the world right there."

After the one-on-one, their advisers joined them for lunch. The president and Kim jovially exchanged compliments and promises neither intended to keep. At one point, the comity was so thick Pompeo wrote something on a notepad and passed it over to Bolton. "He is so full of shit," it read.

Knowing Trump wanted to sign something, Pompeo prepared a short statement for a signing ceremony, but the translators were having trouble resolving language issues, so everyone had to wait. Trump handed out mints to the North Koreans (always selling). He gave Kim signed photos and news clips of the two of them. Trump and Kim then went for a walk in the hotel garden. This was the shot that played over and over again on television sets around the world. Great Theater.

Monopoly

Singapore is a prime example of Trump's belief that, no matter what the situation, he can make a deal. To do that, he is ready to rattle sabers, call out the troops, threaten oil wells, exchange beautiful letters, dial sanctions up or down like a rheostat—"or, hell, just hand me the phone. I'll call the guy myself."

Trump approaches world politics like every country is a piece of real estate on a Monopoly board. He knows all the best countries— China, Russia, India, Japan, Korea, some parts of Europe—but there are a lot of others he couldn't find on a map. Not that they matter. They're probably shitholes anyway.

He especially likes countries run by autocrats. That way, he can put a face on a place, negotiate one-on-one, in private, relying on his grasp of the little things that get deals done.

In one anecdote, Bolton recalls Trump boasting he could solve the whole Iran nuclear problem if he could just get President Hassan Rouhani alone in a room. That nuclear deal it took John Kerry nine months to negotiate? "I could get it done in a day," he said.

NATO

On July 9, Trump set out on a weeklong trip to Europe. First up was the annual meeting of NATO in Brussels, then a state visit to Britain, and finally, a summit with Putin in Helsinki. The president was on a roll when left, buoyed by good press over his new Supreme Court nominee, Brett Kavanaugh. "The family is right out of central casting," Trump crowed.

His first meeting was a breakfast with NATO Secretary-General Jens Stoltenberg. But Stoltenberg couldn't get a word in edgewise in the "tsunami of words" Trump dumped on him. The president started out by complaining that NATO member contributions were a joke. Its new $500 million headquarters building was an extravagance. He was unhappy, very unhappy with the European Union. Its president Jean-Claude Juncker was "a vicious man who hated the United States."

Everyone in NATO hates us, Trump went on. Our allies laugh behind our back when we're not around. Ukraine is corrupt. Obama never should have let Russia take Crimea. And we're supposed to start World War III over Macedonia? They don't even pay their dues. But Trump didn't want to leave any hard feelings, so he concluded, "We're with NATO one hundred percent."

Secretary of Defense James Mattis, who has to deal with all the NATO principals, leaned over and whispered to Bolton, "This is getting pretty silly." In his first bilateral with Germany's Angela Merkel, she asked Trump what he planned to say to Putin. Trump said he had no agenda.

At his next meeting with Emmanuel Macron, the French president wanted to know what Trump's endgame was in his trade wars with China and Europe. It didn't matter, Trump answered. And on it went. The president was not in the mood to make friends.

The next morning, Bolton got a call from Trump. "Are you ready to play in the big leagues today? This is what I want to say. We have great respect for NATO, but we're being treated unfairly. By January 1, all nations must commit to two percent, and we will forgive arrears, or we will walk out, and not defend those who have not. So long as we are not getting along with Russia, we will not go into a NATO where NATO countries are paying billions to Russia. We're out if they make the pipeline deal."

As the leaders gathered around the North Atlantic Council table, Trump motioned Bolton over. "Are we going to do it?" he asked. Bolton replied it was okay to press other countries on paying their fair share, but he shouldn't threaten to walk out. "So, go up to the line, but don't cross it," Bolton warned.

That was like taking a kid to the front door of Willie Wonka's chocolate factory and telling him he can't go in. Trump got all his thoughts out on the table in his usual jumble, since he was just making it up as he went. It was such a jumble of disconnected words that the other NATO leaders called an impromptu meeting afterwards to figure out what he meant. (And yes, he crossed the line.)

But on Air Force One, Trump gave a positive spin to the day's events. "Great success at NATO! Billions of additional dollars paid by members since my election. Great spirit!" he tweeted.

Helsinki

After a visit with the Queen and night at his golf course in Scotland, Trump flew to Helsinki. He was watching a soccer match on the airplane when Bolton tried to brief him for his first meeting with Putin. The Mueller team had just indicted 12 Russian intelligence agents for meddling in the 2016 election, and many members of Congress wanted Trump to demand they be returned to stand trial in the United States.

Trump and Bolton both thought that was a bad idea, first because the U.S. and Russia didn't have an extradition treaty, and second because the odds of it happening were infinitesimal. Bolton suggested Trump say something like, "I'd love to have them come to the United States to prove their innocence." Trump liked it but didn't use it.

When Trump and Putin finally had their sit-down, they talked for almost two hours. Only the principals and interpreters were in the room. No one was allowed to take notes. The U.S. interpreter later confirmed that Putin did 90% of the talking, "which was a switch," Bolton writes.

At the press conference afterwards, Trump read a statement. Putin read a statement. Putin admitted to a reporter that he wanted Trump to win the 2016 election "because he talked about bringing the U.S.-Russian relationship back to normal." They were almost out of the woods when an American reporter asked Trump whether he believed Putin's denials.

"My people came to me—Dan Coats came to me and some others—they said they think it's Russia," Trump shrugged. "I have President Putin. He just said it's not Russia. I will say this: I don't see any reason why it would be, but I really do want to see the server. I have confidence in both parties. So I have great confidence in my intelligence people, but I will tell you that President Putin was extremely strong and powerful in his denial today."

Kelly and Bolton froze in their seats. This was going to require some damage control back home. "Shock waves are rolling across Washington,"

Dan Coats, the director of national intelligence, told Bolton when he reached him on Air Force One. Coats read Bolton a statement the intelligence community wanted to make defending its work. Bolton suggested some changes, but Coats insisted it be released as is, adding fuel to a fire Trump had been fanning for months that the Russia investigation was a hoax.

Ukraine

John Bolton took a lot of heat for not appearing before the House Judiciary Committee when it was considering impeaching the president. In his mind, the politics of impeachment were so poisoned by partisanship his version of events wouldn't have made a difference. No House Republicans were likely to vote for impeachment and, ultimately, it would take 67 senators to impeach. Any insight he might be able to offer, he thought, would have been swallowed up in the preening and posturing of congressmen trying to take full advantage of their five minutes in the limelight.

But he knew Trump was holding back $250 million in military aid to Ukraine until Ukraine's new president, Volodymyr Zelensky, announced an investigation into Hunter Biden. He was, after all, in the room when Trump made the infamous "perfect" telephone call to Zelensky. He had the receipts. They'd talked about it. At least eight times, before and after the phone call, Bolton, Pompeo and Defense Secretary Mark Esper had tried to get Trump to release the money.

Bolton first stepped into the Ukrainian mess on March 25 when he went to see the president in the Oval Office. "I found him in his small dining room with Rudy Giuliani and Jay Sekulow [another of Trump's private attorneys] obviously enjoying discussing the reaction to Mueller's report on his Russian investigation."

Giuliani was there to report in on the latest news from Ukraine. The upstart TV comedian Zelensky had just topped the field in the country's presidential election and was headed to a resounding victory in the April 21 runoff. Giuliani had convinced himself that the Ukrainians, not the Russians, were the chief meddler in the American elections—on behalf of

Hillary Clinton—and the evidence was on a hacked DNC server secreted away somewhere in the Ukraine.

Giuliani also thought it was pretty fishy that Hunter Biden, Joe Biden's son, was getting $83,000 a month to sit on the board of the Ukrainian oil company Burisma, but he told Trump the U.S. Ambassador Marie Yovanovitch was thwarting his efforts to find out more. "She's been bad-mouthing you," Giuliani said, which was all Trump needed to hear.

Don't Badmouth the President

Two days after Zelensky's victory, Trump told Bolton he wanted Yovanovitch fired, "no ifs, ands or buts." (She was recalled May 7.) On June 25—a month before the Zelensky phone call—Trump was talking with Bolton and for the first time raised the idea he could withhold military aid until Giuliani got his meeting with Zelensky.

In Bolton's eyes, Giuliani was "a hand grenade who's going to blow everybody up." By putting the unfounded idea in Trump's head that Ukraine harbored secrets about his political opponent, Giuliani was now jeopardizing $250 million in military aid Congress had authorized for Ukraine to fight off Russian-backed rebels in its eastern provinces.

The money was earmarked for anti-tank weapons, sniper rifles, grenade launchers, night vision goggles, radar, electronic detection devices and medical equipment. If the Trump administration didn't spend it before Sept. 30, the congressional authorization would expire.

Trump didn't particularly care. "I don't want to have any fucking thing to do with Ukraine," he told a delegation that had just returned from Zelensky's inauguration. "They tried to fuck me. They're corrupt. I'm not fucking with them."

The Trump-Zelensky call, Bolton says, was just another brick in the wall Giuliani was building to force an investigation into Hunter Biden. "The linkage of the military assistance with the Giuliani fantasies was already baked in."

Bolton tried to get Attorney General William Barr to tell Trump it was impermissible to leverage U.S governmental authorities for personal political gain, but the president was adamant. In late August, Bolton was scheduled to visit Ukraine, Moldova, Belarus and Poland to shore up their mutual defenses. The visit would end in Warsaw at a ceremony commemorating the 80th anniversary of the German invasion of Poland. Both Trump and Zelensky were slated to attend.

Kurt Volker, the U.S. ambassador to NATO, greeted Bolton with news Zelensky had no wish to get involved in U.S. politics. The Ukrainians had more pressing concerns like cleaning up their own internal corruption, reforming the military in the middle of an armed conflict with Russia, and building a coalition in the new parliament. Giuliani's fantasies were the last thing on Zelensky's mind. Trump would have to raise the issue himself in Warsaw.

Because of Hurricane Dorian's approach to Florida, Trump did not go to Warsaw. He sent Vice President Pence in his stead. From reports later, Bolton heard that Zelensky "homed in on the security package. Pence danced around it, but the lack of a 'yes, it's definitely coming' statement was impossible to hide."

On Labor Day weekend, the president planned a secret meeting with the Taliban at Camp David to sign an Afghan peace agreement. When the press got wind of it, he had to call it off, and he was furious. That Monday, he called Bolton to the Oval Office to say the press coverage made him look like a fool.

"A lot of people don't like you," Trump told Bolton. "They say you're a leaker and not a team player." Bolton demurred. All Trump had to do, he said, was check his press notices to see he was not a press favorite.

"You have your own airplane!" Trump bellowed. "You've got all your own people down there" who are part of a "deep state" trying to sabotage him.

"If you want me to leave, I'll leave," Bolton responded.

"Let's talk about it in the morning," Trump said.

Bolton returned to his office and asked his secretary to put his resignation letter on Trump's desk. "And with that, I was a free man." Bolton writes.

Trump Declassified

There's more in Bolton's book on Ukraine, China, Iran, the whole panoply of foreign affairs the United States conducts every day. Tidbits of nuttiness abound on every page. So it's no wonder the Trump administration tried to stop its publication on the grounds that it has classified material.

"I consider every conversation with me, as president, classified," Trump told reporters. They're not, but maybe they should be. The things that come out of Trump's mouth are appalling, and in a world where your word is your bond, they make you realize this country is being held together right now by Silly Putty.

— August 1, 2020

Live by the Tweet, Die by the Tweet

ABOUT A YEAR INTO THE TRUMP ADMINISTRATION, I stopped writing my column and took to Twitter. Why not? Everyone was doing it, not the least, the president. He was firing off tweets like he was popping amphetamines, usually in the early hours of the morning. So I dove right in.

Twitter was like a giant swimming pool of amorphous thoughts, and we were all playing water polo in the shallow end. You stretch a plastic cap over your brain and swim around in Trump's world, popping up occasionally to take a shot.

On Twitter, there's no time to say anything substantive, so you just skip the story and get right to the punchline. Or find a funny picture and add a snarky caption. If it doesn't make any sense, don't worry, it will slide down the digital drain fast enough.

So here are some of my tweets from 2018. Not all of them. God knows, nobody has time for that.

Stump Connolly
@stumpconnolly

See you there.

10:37 AM - 31 Dec 2017

Stump Connolly
@stumpconnolly

Big trouble brewing in the second grade.

Donald J. Trump ✔
@realDonaldTrump

North Korean Leader Kim Jong Un just stated that the "Nuclear Button is on his desk at all times." Will someone from his depleted and food starved regime please inform him that I too have a Nuclear Button, but it is a much bigger & more powerful one than his, and my Button works!

7:34 PM - 2 Jan 2018

Stump Connolly
@stumpconnolly

Duck and Cover.

CDC to hold briefing on how public can prepare for nuclear war

CDC to hold briefing on how public can prepare for nuclear war
This comes amid rising tensions between the U.S. and North Korea
cbsnews.com

1:22 PM - 5 Jan 2018

Stump Connolly
@stumpconnolly

Just a reminder that, after Trump transferred into Penn (for the undergraduate Wharton degree, not the acclaimed MBA) our "very stable genius" graduated middle of his class. No Summa, no Magna, not even a Cum.

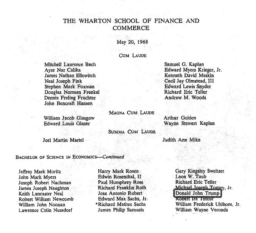

Stump Connolly
@stumpconnolly

Timothy Egan says there are four kinds of Trump supporters:

1) The look-the-other-way evangelicals
2) The get-yours-while-you-can corporate class
3) The ditch-your-principles Republicans
4) and the I'm with Stupids.

7:12 AM - 27 Apr 2018

♡   ↻   ♡ 1   �

Stump Connolly
@stumpconnolly

Will Donald Trump just pick one lie, and stick with it.

2:09 PM - 31 May 2018

♡   ↻   ♡   ili

Stump Connolly
@stumpconnolly

Seven thumbs and seven asses. What do you suppose they should do next?

Donald J. Trump @
@realDonaldTrump

Honored to have Republican Congressional Leadership join me at the @WhiteHouse this evening. Lots to discuss as we continue MAKING AMERICA GREAT AGAIN!

5:59 PM - 11 Apr 2018

Stump Connolly
@stumpconnolly

Land of the Free, Home of the Whites.

Eric Trump @
@EricTrump

Memorial Day at @TrumpNationalNY 🇺🇸🇺🇸 🇺🇸

5:18 AM - 29 May 2018 from The Pool At Trump National Golf Club

Stump Connolly
@stumpconnolly

North Korea remains defiant, but NFL owners cave like a Florida sinkhole.

9:51 AM - 24 May 2018

Stump Connolly
@stumpconnolly

Are you tired of winning yet?

10:16 AM - 11 Jan 2019

Stump Connolly
@stumpconnolly

Donald Trump is not running the federal government. He is running his mouth, and the federal government is trying to keep up.

4:44 PM - 24 Jun 2018

Stump Connolly
@stumpconnolly

There will be a summit. Nothing significant will happen. Trump will call it the greatest diplomatic victory in the history of the world. and Pyongyang will get a new McDonald's.

8:12 AM - 1 Jun 2018

Stump Connolly
@stumpconnolly

"Two men . . . Two leaders . . . One destiny."

White House video presented to Kim Jung Un at Summit. https://youtu.be/Y3EBABDEPkk

6:55 AM - 11 Jun 2018

Stump Connolly
@stumpconnolly

Well, that settles that. All it took was a little Trumpian charm offensive.

Donald J. Trump ✓
@realDonaldTrump

Just landed - a long trip, but everybody can now feel much safer than the day I took office. There is no longer a Nuclear Threat from North Korea. Meeting with Kim Jong Un was an interesting and very positive experience. North Korea has great potential for the future!

7:17 AM - 13 Jun 2018

Stump Connolly
@stumpconnolly

Trump off on BADWILL tour of NATO, London and Helsinki.

6:18 PM - 11 July 2018

Stump Connolly
@stumpconnolly

Is he gone yet?

3:23 PM - 16 July 2018

Stump Connolly
@stumpconnolly

Inside the Trump-Putin Summit: So first things first, Vlad. Do you still have the pee tape?

9:36 PM - 14 July 2018

Stump Connolly
@stumpconnolly

It doesn't get more bonkers than this. Where can I buy the book?

Gina Loudon: "My book actually uses science and real data and true psychological theory to explain why it is quite possible that this president is the most sound minded person to ever occupy the White House."

GINA LOUDON
PRESIDENT TRUMP'S MEDIA ADVISORY BOARD MEMBER
FOX NEWS ALERT
WARN THAT MOVE WILL WORSEN RELATIONS BETWEEN THE COUNTRIES

10:00 PM - 5 Sep 2018

Stump Connolly
@stumpconnolly

It's fruitcake day in Bedminster.

Donald J. Trump ✓
@realDonaldTrump

The Fake News hates me saying that they are the Enemy of the People only because they know it's TRUE. I am providing a great service by explaining this to the American People. They purposely cause great division & distrust. They can also cause War! They are very dangerous & sick!

9:50 AM - 5 Aug 2018

Stump Connolly
@stumpconnolly

one paragraph, six lies.

Mark MacKinnon ✓
@markmackinnon

Follow

On Donald Trump and the truth (from @peterbakernyt and @YLindaQiu):

> He has asserted that construction has begun on his border wall (it has not), that he is one of the most popular American presidents in history (he is not), that he "always" opposed the Iraq war (he did not), that the stock market reopened the day after the terrorist attacks of Sept. 11, 2001 (it did not), that his tax cut was the largest in history (it was not) and that the United States is the only country that guarantees citizenship to those born here (it is not).

3:12 AM - 2 Nov 2018

Stump Connolly
@stumpconnolly

Who ever saw that coming?

Bloomberg Politics @bpolitics
North Korea says it will not give up nuclear weapons unless the U.S. removes its nuclear threat first bloom.bg/2CokGMt

1:12 AM - 20 Dec 2018

Stump Connolly
@stumpconnolly

Watch out. The immigrant invaders are pulling out the heavy artillery. Will 15,000 troops be enough?

Trump is lying to scare voters. Migrant caravan families are desperate, not te...
Families running for their lives are not a terrorist threat. And Trump's 'solutions,' like cutting off aid and deploying the military, will create chaos.
usatoday.com

9:14 AM - 25 Oct 2018

Stump Connolly
@stumpconnolly

Yeah, I do that all the time.

Sarah Westwood
@sarahcwestwood

President Trump accuses people of changing their clothes and returning to cast additional ballots in disguise. (there's no evidence of this) "Sometimes they go to their car, put on a different hat, put on a different shirt, come in and vote again."

8:39 AM - 15 Nov 2018

Stump Connolly
@stumpconnolly

I'm most thankful for me. And you should be too.

Ram Ramgopal ✓
@RamCNN

Trump wrapped up his telephone call with troops and questions with reporters at Mar-a-Lago with this:

Reporter: What are you most thankful for, Mr. President?

Trump: For having a great family and for having made a tremendous difference in this country. I made a tremendous difference in the country. This country is so much stronger now than it was when I took office that you won't believe it. And I mean, you see it, but so much stronger that people can't even believe it. When I see foreign leaders, they say we cannot believe the difference in strength between the United States now and the United States two years. ago. Made a lot of progress.

Thank you, everybody.

3:10 PM - 22 Nov 2018

Stump Connolly
@stumpconnolly

But who's counting?

Josh Dawsey ✓ @jdawsey1
By the end of the year, Trump had accumulated more than 7,600 untruths during his presidency – averaging more than 15 erroneous claims a day in 2018.

5:56 AM - 13 Jan 2019

🗨 1   🔁   ♡   ili

Stump Connolly
@stumpconnolly

Mr. President, you're holding it upside down.

Donald J. Trump ✓
@realDonaldTrump

Christmas Eve briefing with my team working on North Korea – Progress being made. Looking forward to my next summit with Chairman Kim!

3:14 PM - 24 Dec 2018

◯   ⟲   ♡ 1   ıll

Stump Connolly
@stumpconnolly

Hegemony: Money from a hedge fund.

Craig Newman ✓ @craignewman
Who gets to tell the president what hegemony means? twitter.com/IlvesToomas/st...

3:39 PM - 19 Oct 2018

◯   ⟲   ♡ 1   ıll

Stump Connolly
@stumpconnolly

You're going to give the chairman of the Fed putting lessons on the economy? Four bankruptcies say that's not going to work out well.

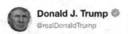

Donald J. Trump ✔
@realDonaldTrump

The only problem our economy has is the Fed. They don't have a feel for the Market, they don't understand necessary Trade Wars or Strong Dollars or even Democrat Shutdowns over Borders. The Fed is like a powerful golfer who can't score because he has no touch - he can't putt!

10:23 AM - 24 Dec 2018

Stump Connolly
@stumpconnolly

Who ever saw this coming?

Jim Tankersley ✔
@jimtankersley

It's Official: The Trump tax cuts didn't pay for themselves in Year One: federal tax revenues declined in 2018 while economic growth accelerated, undercutting the Trump administration's insistence that the $1.5 trillion tax package would pay for itself.

nytimes.com

9:38 AM - 12 Jan 2019

○   ⟳   ♡   ᵢₗᵢ

Stump Connolly
@stumpconnolly

I AM NOT A SNITCH!

3:42 PM - 25 Jan 2019

Stump Connolly
@stumpconnolly

Thought for the Day: Trump Presidential Library.

8:27 AM - 10 Jan 2019

Shipwreck

Keeping Score

THE ECONOMIC SHUTDOWN brought on by the coronavirus pandemic led to a loss of 20 million jobs in April, so it's no wonder President Trump was happy to see May, and the 2.5 million jobs that came back with it. It was the first sign the economy is on the rebound. But Friday's unemployment report deserves closer scrutiny.

Fifty-five percent of those jobs (1.4 million) were in the bar and restaurant business. Those jobs would have come back whether America "reopened" on May 1, as Trump insisted, or June 1, the beginning of a phased recovery favored by the Coronavirus Task Force.

Another 464,000 jobs (18%) were in construction. If you can't build in the summer, when can you? And let's give Trump credit for the 225,000-job increase in manufacturing, but let's also thank GM, Ford and Chrysler for reopening their assembly lines.

The 312,000 people who came back to work in the health care sector reflects the fact that, duh, they were responding to a certain crisis that required their attention. But those gains were offset by the layoff of another 585,000 government employees in May.

In its 14 categories of employment, the Bureau of Labor Statistics identified five where the employment numbers were down: government, banking, warehousing, utilities and media. If you are looking at the numbers as a reporter, you might say your chances of getting rehired are about as good as a snowball in hell these days. Welcome to retirement!

Yes, the unemployment rate dropped from 14% to 13%. Most of that came from white workers going back to work. But black unemployment didn't budge an inch. Among black teens, unemployment in May actually rose from 28% to 35%. And you wonder why the knee on the neck of George Floyd is something more than a case of police misbehavior?

Our health and economy are inextricably bound together. The numbers can be twisted to make any political point. The unemployment rate, the cases of COVID-19, and anything that comes out of the president's mouth is suspect.

Any interpretation of the numbers you don't like is branded fake news. But the facts are another 10,000 Americans died of COVID-19 last week. The number of Americans infected is now approaching 2 million. States that reopened early are reporting an increase in coronavirus cases. The effect of protesters marching without masks won't be measurable until two weeks from now.

As much as I'd like to drink in public again without a mask, I somehow think we are not out of the woods.

— June 6, 2020

To Mask or Not to Mask

FOR A MAN WITH A LOT OF OPINIONS, I'm pretty easygoing when it comes to managing my own life. I like to think I'm young at heart, but I'm not. Parenthood—in the form of three boys—has taught me otherwise. Now I'm fond of saying, "With age comes wisdom."

One of the ways wisdom comes in handy is during an epidemic. Young people seem to think COVID-19 will never happen to them. Wisdom teaches you, "Never say never." That doesn't mitigate—the word of the moment—my desire to walk around without a mask, drink in bars, enjoy lunch at restaurants with my friends, or otherwise act like we are living in normal times. I just don't, for the time being.

I've long believed in the right of individuals to do whatever they want. Okay, so you can't shout "Fire!" in a crowded theater. The right to bear arms probably doesn't cover pulling a tank up into your front driveway. And it's okay to pay taxes, even though it's obviously a socialist scheme to redistribute the wealth. But I've had my share of encounters with government bureaucrats demanding I get a permit to put an addition on my house, plant flowers in the parkway or build a fence around my garbage cans.

There are 14,000 pages of regulations in the federal registry, and I can't believe we need them all. But I don't object to one more: wear a mask. I don't know how long we will need it, or whether it's even going to make a difference in the spread of the virus, but another lesson that comes with age is "Better safe than sorry."

Smarter people than me—and I don't include Donald Trump in that category—watch the COVID-19 death toll pass 150,000 and say the best way to stop the spread of this infectious disease is to wear a mask.

I have no reason to doubt them, and neither does Donald Trump. Trump boasts (falsely) that America's mortality rate is one of the lowest in the world. It is not. Like war, COVID-19 isn't all about the deaths, but also the casualties. Everyone who went into the hospitals and, thankfully, came out not dead.

I don't wear a mask because I'm a health nut. I don't even wear one all the time. Neighborhood kids are running in and out of my house every day without a mask, and my front stoop is a frequent gathering spot for their parents (who also don't wear masks). In another new term the coronavirus experts have given us, this is my summer cohort. My neighbors.

But when I go to the grocery store, I wear a mask. When I walk in or out of a restaurant, I wear a mask. I wash my hands more often than I used to. I've stopped shaking hands with friends. And every time I plan to see a friend, I ask myself how many potential carriers he's exposed himself to. Did he wear a mask?

I'm not as diligent as I probably should be. But this isn't a political issue. It's not a question of my right not to wear a mask. It's my way of protecting my friends from me, and me from them. And with every right comes a responsibility.

Use common sense.

Wear a mask.

— July 24, 2020

The Press Conference

WITH ONLY ONE QUESTION ON THE PUBLIC'S MIND—how do we get out of this coronavirus mess?—President Trump held a press conference Tuesday to talk about anything but.

In just over an hour, he spent 52 minutes in a long soliloquy that Peter Baker, of *The New York Times*, called "an hour of presidential stream of consciousness."

He spoke, in no particular order, about China, Joe Biden (22 times), a big day in the stock market ("things are coming back, and they're coming back very rapidly"), the World Trade Organization ("one of the greatest geopolitical and economic disasters in world history"), the World Health Organization (a terrible deal), and the Paris climate accord (a disaster).

He went on to give us his opinion of America's crumbling highways, tariffs, the census, mail-in voting, his beautiful wall and the U.S. military ("We have the best tanks, the best ships, the best missiles, rockets. We have the best of everything.")

And that was just the first 10 minutes. He then veered off to lambaste Biden's son Hunter for sitting on the board of the Ukrainian oil company Burisma, Barack Obama for allowing China "to pillage our factories, plunder our communities and steal our most precious secrets," and Biden (again) for economic policies that will "destroy our country."

Random Thoughts Without the Thought

"Mr. Trump drifted seemingly at random from one topic to another, often in the same run-on sentence," Baker wrote. "Even for a president who rarely sticks to the script and wanders from thought to thought, it was one of the most rambling performances of his presidency."

Baker wasn't the only reporter to notice. "Trump Pivots to Self-Pity" headlined *Bloomberg News*. "President Donald Trump swept to power by championing the hardships of forgotten men and women, but his re-election bid has so far centered on the plight of just one person: himself."

"What you saw was a man without a plan," Charlie Sykes, the conservative Milwaukee radio commentator, told Nicolle Wallace. "He didn't seem to care, didn't seem connected to reality, and displayed no sense of empathy whatsoever."

Trump made familiar stops along the way at all the things he's done to keep the coronavirus under control. His ban on travel from China, his respirators, naming Mike Pence to run the Coronavirus Task Force. "He works so hard and gets so little credit," Trump said. "We'd be on the phone with 50 different governors who'd all tell us what a great job we did. And then they'll go to the media and say, 'Well, they didn't do such a good job.' Well, we did a great job."

But the president made no mention of the surge of cases in Florida, Texas, Arizona, Georgia and other states that reopened early on his urging. He repeated his false claim that the U.S. mortality rate from COVID-19 is among the lowest in the world (in fact, it is sixth highest per capita), and again pushed to get children back in school when 62% of parents consider the schools unsafe.

Biden Baiting

Just when it looked like the press might be able to ask a question, Trump jumped off on another 20-minute tangent about Joe Biden giving in to the radical left. This was not a spur-of-the-moment digression. He had talking points on a piece of paper in front of him that the White House opposition research team had massaged out of Biden's Unity Meeting with Bernie Sanders.

Each was couched in an inflammatory cliche. By Trump's reckoning, Biden will kill American energy, abolish law enforcement, promote human trafficking, free violent criminals, give welfare to illegal aliens, close prisons, abolish our police departments, end school choice, erase educational standards, make home prices in the suburbs drop like a rock, and tear down statues honoring George Washington, Andrew Jackson, Abraham Lincoln and the Emancipation Proclamation.

Daniel Dale, the CNN fact-checker who was following along on Twitter, counted 19 false or misleading statements before he gave up. "I'm no longer live-tweeting because Trump is lying so much I keep having to stop."

"People are feeling good about our country," Trump went on. But they aren't. The latest Gallup poll says 38% of Americans approve of the job Trump is doing, and 57% do not.

But speaking of polls, Trump wanted to point out that Barack Obama and Joe Biden "got very poor marks from Gallup for the job they did on swine flu." Except that too is false. A Gallup poll taken at the height of the 2009 swine flu epidemic showed only 13% of Americans were worried about getting it and 87% were not. And Obama's approval rating at the time was 66%. Ratings be damned, 1,469 Americans died from swine flu—a tragedy to be sure but not close to the coronavirus death toll.

Rhetorical Mustard

"Because of his incontinent use of it, the rhetorical mustard that the president slathers on every subject has lost its tang," George Will, not exactly a flaming liberal, noted. "The entertainer has become a bore, and foretelling his defeat no longer involves peering into a distant future."

"We are down to Kool-Aid drinkers and next of kin at the White House," CNN's Jim Acosta noted. "There are no adults here who can level with the president and tell him he can't deliver a rally-like rant in the Rose Garden."

Press conferences are a chance for reporters to get the president's response to events of the day. The give-and-take sharpens the thinking of both and illuminates the public. In this case, the president was all give and no take. He took only four questions in six minutes. The last, obviously planted by the White House, came from a sympathetic OAN reporter who wondered whether the Railroad Retirement Board should take Trump's advice not to invest in Chinese weapons manufacturers.

But the good news? "We will be having these conferences again," he promised the reporters.

— July 16, 2020

Shoe on the
Other Foot

Put into the category of what-goes-around-comes-around the recent nomination of Amy Coney Barrett to fill Ruth Bader Ginsberg's seat on the Supreme Court. In the last year of President Obama's term, he nominated a distinguished member of the U.S Court of Appeals in Washington, Merrick Garland, to fill the seat of Antonin Scalia.

Justice Scalia died in February of 2016. Obama nominated Garland in March, eight months before the November election, but the Republicans in the Senate refused to even consider him.

"The American people should have a voice in the selection of their next Supreme Court justice," Mitch McConnell, the Senate majority leader, proclaimed. "Therefore, this vacancy should not be filled until we have a new president." And that was pretty much that, except for all the speechifying the Republicans did to support him. So let's take a look at what some of them said:

Sen. Cory Gardner (Colo.): "I think we're too close to the election. The president who is elected in November should be the one who makes this decision."

Sen. Ron Johnson (Wis.): "I strongly agree that the American people should decide the future direction of the Supreme Court by their votes for president and the majority party in the U.S. Senate."

Sen. John Cornyn (Texas): "I believe the American people deserve to have a voice in the selection of the next Supreme Court Justice, and the best way to ensure that happens is to have the Senate consider a nomination made by the next President."

Sen. Ted Cruz (Texas): "It has been 80 years since a Supreme Court vacancy was nominated and confirmed in an election year. There is a long tradition that you don't do this in an election year."

Sen. Lindsey Graham (S.C.): "If an opening comes in the last year of President Trump's term, and the primary process has started, we'll wait to the next election."

Sen. Marco Rubio (Fla.): "I don't think we should be moving on a nominee in the last year of this president's term—I would say that if it was a Republican president."

Sen. Jim Inhofe (Okla.): "It makes the current presidential election all that more important as not only are the next four years in play, but an entire generation of Americans will be impacted by the balance of the court and its rulings...I will oppose this nomination as I firmly believe we must let the people decide the Supreme Court's future."

Sen. Chuck Grassley (Iowa): "A lifetime appointment that could dramatically impact individual freedoms and change the direction of the court for at least a generation is too important to get bogged down in politics. The American people shouldn't be denied a voice."

Sen. Joni Ernst (Iowa): "We will see what the people say this fall and our next president, regardless of party, will be making that nomination."

Sen. Thom Tillis (N.C.): "The campaign is already under way. It is essential to the institution of the Senate and to the very health of our republic to not launch our nation into a partisan, divisive confirmation battle during the very same time the American people are casting their ballots to elect our next president."

Sen. David Perdue (Ga.): "The very balance of our nation's highest court is in serious jeopardy. As a member of the Senate Judiciary Committee, I will do everything in my power to encourage the president and Senate leadership not to start this process until we hear from the American people."

Sen. Pat Toomey (Pa.): "The next Court appointment should be made by the newly-elected president."

Sen. Richard Burr (N.C.): "In this election year, the American people will have an opportunity to have their say in the future direction of our country. For this reason, I believe the vacancy left open by Justice Antonin Scalia should not be filled until there is a new president."

Sen. Roy Blunt (Mo.): "The Senate should not confirm a new Supreme Court justice until we have a new president."

Sen. John Hoeven (N.D.): "There is 80 years of precedent for not nominating and confirming a new justice of the Supreme Court in the final year of a president's term so that people can have a say in this very important decision."

Sen. Rob Portman (Ohio): "I believe the best thing for the country is to trust the American people to weigh in on who should make a lifetime appointment that could reshape the Supreme Court for generations."

Now jump ahead four years to Justice Ginsberg's death in September. President Trump waited eight days before he nominated Barrett, a Chicago appellate court judge, on Sept. 26, and McConnell is pushing to get her confirmed before the November election.

If you think principles are required to be a member of the United States Senate, think again.

— September 26, 2020

The End is Near

Never in Doubt

I BARELY HAD TIME TO GET THE MAALOX DOWN MY THROAT on election night before it came vomiting up the next morning in a deluge of mail-in ballots.

Overnight, President Trump's lead in Wisconsin, Michigan, Arizona and Nevada vanished, and it appeared Joe Biden would have enough votes in the Electoral College to win the presidency. But they were still counting.

Turnout for this election was in the neighborhood of 155 million—the highest in American history. Nearly 100 million of the voters have taken advantage of early voting or mail-in ballots to participate. But in all but a dozen states, election officials were barred from opening the mail-in ballots until Election Day.

Most of the voters who actually went to the polls on Election Day were Republicans, the "red wave" prompted by President Trump's constant warnings that mail-in votes were unreliable. After those votes were banked, election officials moved on to the mail-in ballots, creating a "blue shift" in the tally since roughly two-thirds of those ballots favored Biden.

If you wonder why in-person votes on Election Day came in fast and mail-ins were slow, remember there were more of them, and counting the mail-ins is a painstaking task. Each envelope needs to be checked for a postmark and valid signature, slit open, sorted by hand to the appropriate precinct, then entered into the tally, thus requiring huge counting rooms in major cities and thousands of additional poll workers, many in states that have never done mail-in voting.

By midnight, the networks had called the outcome in only 30 states. Watching the returns come in from the White House, the president exploded when Fox News called Arizona for Biden. He made Jared Kushner call his friend Rupert Murdoch to demand that Fox News take it back. What good that would do is hard to fathom. But the president's mind was racing. The optics were bad.

'An Embarrassment to Our Country'

At 2:30 a.m., still fuming, he assembled about 100 diehard supporters to a press conference in the East Room. His family occupied the front row. Only one mask could be seen in the audience.

"We were getting ready for a big celebration," he said. "We were winning everywhere, and all of a sudden it was just called off." He ticked off his current vote margins in states with millions of votes yet to be counted. Then he demanded the election be deemed over.

"This is a fraud on the American public. This is an embarrassment to our country. We were getting ready to win this election. Frankly, we did win the election. We want all voting to stop."

He vowed to take his case to the Supreme Court, but since they were not in session, he took his case to Twitter to carry on the fight in the only arena that accommodates stupid people.

"We are up BIG, but they are trying to STEAL the Election," he tweeted at 2:45 a.m. "We will never let them do it. Votes cannot be cast after the Poles [sic] are closed!" But he was not done. "How come every time they count Mail-In ballot dumps they are so devastating in their percentage and power of destruction?" he tweeted again.

Over the course of the night, he would tweet 20 more times, but Twitter blocked most of them as false or misleading. "The President's Twitter feed currently has more warnings than a pack of cigarettes," Politico's Washington correspondent Ryan Lizza observed.

When I awoke Wednesday morning, Trump was still at it. "Last night I was leading, often solidly, in many key States, in almost all instances Democrat run & controlled. Then, one by one, they started to magically disappear as surprise ballot dumps were counted."

Indeed, while we slept, Biden had closed the gap in the battleground states of Wisconsin and Michigan. Georgia, North Carolina, Pennsylvania and Nevada remained too close to call. This gave Biden a 243 to 214 edge in the Electoral College. But neither candidate was close to the 270 votes needed to win.

The Magic Wall

The news channels had prepared themselves for a long vote count that could take two or three days, so it was all hands on deck Wednesday morning as they waited for the votes to come in. There were reporters galore outside the counting rooms. Campaign spokesmen bloviated about their prospects. There were tally board graphics for each state to track votes as they were tabulated. But the weapon of choice in the newsrooms was the Magic Wall.

The Magic Wall was introduced to politics in the 2008 presidential race by CNN's John King. A former AP political editor and computer geek with 30 years of experience on the campaign trail, he uses it to draw on his encyclopedic knowledge of state politics. He hopscotches across the electoral map, clicking on battleground states, zooming in on key counties, and comparing vote totals from previous elections. His commentary is a civics lesson in a math class—with a dizzying array of possible outcomes based on votes yet to be counted.

Steve Kornacki on MSNBC is a worthy rival. With a little panache, and a lot more enthusiasm, he fast-fingers his way across the board like it's an Xbox controller. But King is the master.

After the first of many such sessions at the wall Wednesday morning, King turned plaintively to the camera. "All day we'll be sweeping across the country checking on the battleground states. How many votes are out? Where are they? And there will be recounts. So the operative word here is patience. We're just going to have to let them count the votes."

Exit Polls

The other go-to feature on election night is the exit polls. Traditionally, exit polls are meticulously conducted in key voting precincts to give viewers a sense of what people are thinking when they cast their ballots. Because so many people didn't vote in their usual precinct, the results this year were suspect. But the data, if you can believe it, showed:

- One in 3 voters said the economy was their biggest concern, 1 in 5 cited racial inequality, and 1 in 6 named the coronavirus pandemic.
- Health care and law and order, the issues that supposedly divided Republicans and Democrats, were top of mind in only 10% of the voters
- And on the question of the day, 70% said they routinely wear masks and 50% believe the U.S. mismanaged the coronavirus crisis.

By age, the exit polls say Biden won heavily in the 18-29 demographic (62%), edged out Trump with middle-aged voters (51%) and almost won the traditionally Republican senior vote (48%).

His support among white voters was 5 points higher than Hillary Clinton's in 2016, but Trump made inroads with black males (10%) and Latinos (32%) while suburban women, perhaps the most prized segment of the electorate this year, went for Biden (56%) over Trump (43%).

Patience

As the day wore on, patience was paying off for the Biden camp. But patience is not one of Donald Trump's long suits.

The president's legal team filed its first lawsuit at 2:45 p.m. Wednesday. It kind of, sort of, asked the Supreme Court to intervene in Pennsylvania, when every other court said it shouldn't. Then Trump's legal team filed another lawsuit challenging vote counts in Michigan, and another in Georgia, and a petition for a recount in Wisconsin.

Trump tried to do his part the only way he knows how. "We hereby claim the State of Michigan if, in fact there was a large number of secretly dumped ballots as has been widely reported!" he tweeted, although by then Michigan was firmly in the Biden column.

The Trump lawsuits were all over the map. He was challenging thousands of ballots in Nevada—not exactly challenging but holding a press conference—without citing any facts. The recount in Wisconsin was on, then off, then on again. He lost an appeal to have Trump poll watchers sit at every counting table in Philadelphia to double-check every mail-in ballot.

Jake Tapper compared the Trump effort to a legal game of whack-a-mole. Jim Acosta quoted a senior White House adviser saying they were going state to state like ambulance chasers, "and to make matters worse, Rudy Giuliani is on the case."

On ABC's evening newscast, Jon Karl explained. "The legal strategy seems to be this. Stopping the count in places where Trump is winning. And keeping the count going where he is behind."

With Trump out stirring the waters, Biden made an attempt to calm them in a press conference Wednesday afternoon in Wilmington. "It's time to put the harsh rhetoric of the campaign behind us, to lower the temperature, to see each other again, to listen to one another, to hear each other again, and respect and care for one another, to unite, to heal, to come together as a nation."

Biden took pains not to look like he was claiming victory. "I'm not here to declare that we've won, but I am here to report when the count is finished, we believe we will be the winners," he said. "Of all the votes counted, we have won Wisconsin by 20,000 votes, virtually the same margin that

President Trump won that state four years ago. In Michigan, we lead by over 35,000 votes. And I feel very good about Pennsylvania. Virtually all the remaining ballots to be counted are cast by mail. And we've been winning 78% of the votes by mail in Pennsylvania."

One Last Fling on the Merry-Go-Round

Thursday morning, Biden met with his coronavirus task force as new cases spiked to 120,000 a day, hospitalizations were at record levels, and the death toll now routinely topped 1,000 people a day.

President Trump, by contrast, woke up Thursday chomping at the bit to get out in public. His campaign team tried everything they could think of to restrain him. They told him Rudy Giuliani and Pam Bondi, his favorite ass kissers, were on the case in Philadelphia. Richard Grenell, his former acting director of national intelligence, and Matt Schlapp, another conservative flack, were in Nevada trying to find the "illegal" votes. And a few Republican senators were coming around to believing his claim that the election was being stolen.

But his hopes to win were unraveling. His lead in Georgia was down to 20,800 votes—out of 5 million cast. The gap in Pennsylvania, where he had a 600,000 plurality on election night, was 108,000—with 370,000 votes still out. The media now routinely counted Nevada and Arizona in Biden's column, and "Sleepy Joe" Biden was strutting around in front of the cameras like a peacock on cocaine.

As the networks prepared for the nightly news shows, the producers got word that the president wanted to go live from the White House briefing room. Trump walked into the room at 5:45 p.m. with a dour face, his shoulders hunched, carrying a sheaf of notes. He stepped to the podium and gave the most malicious, self-serving, defiant and jaw-dropping performance of his administration.

Big Media, Big Money and Big Tech

"Big media, big money and big tech" were conspiring to steal the election from him, he said. The pollsters were in on it. They kept churning out fake numbers "to keep our voters at home, create the illusion of momentum for

Mr. Biden and diminish Republican's ability to raise funds." The Democrats were behind it. All the election officials in the battleground states were Democrats, and they had marching orders to keep counting Biden votes until "our numbers started miraculously getting whittled away in secret."

About five minutes into his speech, ABC, CBS and NBC cut away. "We have to interrupt here," Lester Holt said, "because the president has made a number of false statements, including the notion that there has been fraudulent voting. There has been no evidence of that."

Trump kept rambling on the cable channels. He had a litany of grievance. A corrupt Democratic machine in Philadelphia. "I went to school there and I know a lot about it." Paper covering the windows of a polling station in Detroit (a precaution many states take to keep video cameras from peering in on the ballots). Unexplained delays, mystery ballots, illegal votes, secret counting rooms, and "disturbing irregularities."

At one point, Trump sounded like he was reading all the tweets that Twitter wouldn't let him publish. At another point, you'd have thought he was auditioning for a job as Steve Kornacki's weatherman, standing over his shoulder giving his version of the mood of the nation. "It looks like we have a heavy vote blowing in, partly shady with a chance of fraud."

It was a dark, dangerous, stunningly ungracious speech. He took no questions.

"What a sad night for the United States of America," Jake Tapper said when Trump finished. "To hear their president say that, to falsely accuse people of trying to steal the election, to attack democracy in that way with this feast of falsehood. Lie after lie after lie. Pathetic."

The Mainstream Media Weighs In

"As he was talking, I was reaching out to Republicans to ask when the intervention is going to happen because this isn't just partisan. This isn't just dangerous. It's nonsensical," Dana Bash said in a CNN roundtable discussion that followed.

"This president clearly knows this is not going to end well for him," Abby Phillip added, "and he's trying to take the rest of the country down with him."

"I don't think we've ever seen anything like this from a president of the United States," chimed in Anderson Cooper. "Of course it is dangerous, and, of course, it will go to the courts, but you'll notice the president did not have any evidence, at all. Nothing. That is the president of the United States, one of the most powerful people in the world, and we see him like an obese turtle on his back flailing in the hot sun."

"It is a speech that represents one of the more dangerous acts that Donald Trump has undertaken as president," Nicolle Wallace said on MSNBC. "The country is a tinderbox. A lot of people went out and voted for Donald Trump on Tuesday, and we've heard militia groups, and others, say they will not accept any other decision than a Trump victory. Taking the president's words for what they are, this is the most incendiary, the most dangerous, and the most flagrantly false lie he has told—at a moment when this country is in a fraught state."

Meanwhile, in Alternate Reality

Meanwhile, across the channels, Sean Hannity was trying to make Trump's case for him on Fox. Hannity devoted his prime hour to "an investigative report" for his 4 million viewers into how the Democrats stole the election.

His guest reporters were the same Pam Bondi and Matt Schlapp that Trump's legal team sent to Pennsylvania and Nevada. Their video evidence came from Project Veritas, the right wing, gotcha video group run by James O'Keefe. Its contribution was a lot of shaky footage of Trump flunkies looking through paper-covered windows at people trying to do their job, count the votes.

Hannity couldn't contain his outrage. "Ask yourself, do you trust what you are seeing tonight? Can you believe election returns where everything is shrouded in secrecy?"

After Trump complained that not enough senators were stepping up to defend him, Hannity brought on a few to offer their obeyance.

"He stood by me, so I'm standing by him," Lindsey Graham said. Only a few days earlier, Graham had been on Fox begging money for his South Carolina Senate campaign. Tonight, he pledged $500,000 to President Trump's Legal Defense Fund.

Ted Cruz came on next to decry the outrageous, partisan, political and lawless election workers who have "clouded the vote counting in a shroud of darkness."

But Newt Gingrich topped them all. He demanded Attorney General Bill Barr fire all the election workers in Pennsylvania and have the state legislature throw out the election returns. Now there's a good idea. Throw out the baby, the bathwater and the midwife.

Let's do this all over again next year. What do you say?

Is It Over?

The last of the mail-in ballots were counted on Friday. The tally showed Biden jumped ahead in Pennsylvania, increased his lead in Nevada, was still strong in Arizona, and, in a sign of the changing times, had a razor thin plurality in Georgia, where a Democrat hasn't won since Bill Clinton in 1992.

There is more counting to go: military ballots, provisional ballots, cured ballots, recounts. Under this year's intense scrutiny, election officials want to make sure all the *i*'s are dotted and the *t*'s crossed before their state certifies a winner. But the handwriting is on the wall.

Joe Biden has won the popular vote so far by 4 million votes. (74,487,517 to 70,336,783.) And he is on a glide path to win the Electoral College, 306-232, the same margin Trump called a landslide in 2016.

Trump's victory came on the back of 76,000 votes in three battleground states: Wisconsin (22,000), Michigan (10,000) and Pennsylvania (44,000).

Biden won this year by a similarly narrow 255,000 votes in six battleground states: Wisconsin (20,000), Michigan (148,000), Pennsylvania (35,000), Georgia (7,000), Nevada (25,000) and Arizona (20,000).

Trump says he won't concede. He'll take his case to the highest court in the land. But the Supreme Court justices are smart enough not to muck this up.

And who cares? Trump is out of here.

Joe Biden will be the 46th president of the United States.

Was it ever in doubt?

— November 7, 2020

See You in Court

THE DENOUEMENT OF Donald Trump's presidential campaign came fittingly in the Four Seasons Total Landscaping parking lot outside Philadelphia, between a crematorium and an adult bookstore, at roughly the same time the TV networks were proclaiming Joe Biden the winner. Thus making Donald Trump the loser.

Rudy Giuliani, the captain of Trump's legal team, was at the helm when the ship went down. Trump was on the golf course.

Giuliani was there to announce the Trump campaign would be filing at least a dozen lawsuits to overturn the election outcome. They would all be based on "troubling irregularities" in states Biden won like Michigan, Wisconsin, Pennsylvania, Arizona, Nevada and Georgia.

And the most troubling thing, he said, was that he couldn't see them.

The Evidence

Giuliani had affidavits, *sworn affidavits signed under penalty of perjury,* from poll watchers who witnessed various misdeeds. The greatest travesty took place in the warehouse-size counting centers in Philadelphia and Pittsburgh. Set up to handle the millions of anticipated mail-in ballots—in the middle of a pandemic—election officials kept Trump's poll watchers at least six feet away from the people actually doing the work. Giuliani was outraged.

"Those mail-in ballots could have been from anybody. Those mail-in ballots could have been for anybody they wrote in," he said. "Those mail-in ballots could have been written the day before by the Democratic Party hacks that were all over the Convention Center.

"If you have nothing to hide with these mail-in ballots, you allow inspection. I mean, this is common knowledge, common practice," he went on. "You take out the absentee ballot, you open it up, the Republican looks at it, the Democrat looks at it. If nobody objects, you put it in the pile. If either object, you put it aside." (Leave aside for a minute how long it would take for Rudy's sleuths to inspect Pennsylvania's 2.5 million mail-in ballots this way.) "That is unheard of. It's illegal, it's unconstitutional, and we will be bringing an action challenging that," he said.

How to Steal an Election

The real culprit is the Democratic machine in Philadelphia with a long history of stealing elections, he went on. "You're in a city in which voter fraud is professional. Some places may be amateurs at voter fraud. Philadelphia is a professional place for voter fraud because you have a decrepit Democrat machine that you have had in power for 60 years."

As an old reporter in Chicago, I would like to say a word on behalf of the real professionals. I was a poll watcher in Chicago assigned to an Uptown polling site in 1972. I watched precinct captains chaperone enfeebled old residents of a senior public housing project into buses to get them to the polls, and yes, I saw them enter the sanctity of the polling booth to "assist" the voters pull the lever.

I've seen winos vote in a West Side flophouse, campaign workers tear down yard signs and ward bosses hand out cheat sheets with the party's favorite candidates. One year, to make it simple, they put the whole Democratic ticket on one ballot line and handed out cards that said, PUNCH 10.

This was the way the great Democratic machines stole elections in the past in Chicago, Detroit, Philadelphia, New York and other big cities. With hard work, and style.

But there are no machines left these days. You can't stuff a ballot box, because there are no boxes left to stuff. It's all computer touch screens, early voting, mail-in voting, interconnected eligibility rolls—all supervised by tens of thousands of volunteers, Republicans and Democrats, trying to make democracy work as it was intended.

Buzzwords for the Mill

Giuliani is a creature of this storied past. He knows all the anecdotes and all the buzzwords, even though it's probably been decades since he was in a polling place, or for that matter, arguing a case in court.

It really doesn't matter whether he knows what he is talking about, the buzzwords are grist for Trump's mill. The president's Twitter feed has been grinding them out since election night, and they are having the intended effect. Seventy percent of Republicans now believe the election was not "free and fair," according to a *Politico*/*Morning Call* poll.

And in Washington, the Vichy Republicans in Congress are going along with the charade. Not just the Trump sycophants. No one in the Republican leadership will come right out and say that Trump lost. They are afraid of Trump's wrath, and the lies he may tweet about them someday if *they* become his target.

In private, they are confident there will be a smooth transition. They just want to give the president's bruised ego time a little time to heal. "The president has every right to make every vote count," they say, which maybe the most mealy-mouthed abdication of public responsibility I can imagine.

(Okay, maybe Trump's denial of responsibility for the coronavirus crisis is another. How about Mitch McConnell in the Senate? Mike Pence in hiding? There are so many people abdicating responsibility in Washington these days, it's hard to imagine them all.)

The Devil Is in the Details

So how are Trump's lawsuits coming? Seven have been dismissed out of hand. In the battleground states, here's where we are now:

MICHIGAN. Biden leads in Michigan by 145,000 votes. State judges have dismissed two attempts to delay certification of the results.

"This court finds that while there are assertions made by the plaintiffs that there is no evidence in support of those assertions," one judge ruled.

"On this factual record, I have no basis to find there's a likelihood of success," said the other.

Those rulings, of course, didn't deter the Trump legal team from filing a federal suit in the friendlier U.S. District Court in Grand Rapids Tuesday claiming vote fraud on the other side of the state in Detroit. That too was dismissed.

ARIZONA. Biden leads in Arizona by 14,000 votes. One judge has already rejected a Trump lawsuit claiming that Sharpies in a polling place bled through and ruined ballots. Another is taking under consideration a lawsuit to determine whether poll workers pressed a button to cancel an "overwrite" of a Trump vote. I'll bet that is really keeping him up at night.

"This is just a stalling tactic to delay the official canvass," said Arizona Secretary of State Katie Hobbs. "They are grasping at straws."

But hundreds of Trump supporters nonetheless rallied in downtown Phoenix Saturday to denounce the media conspiracy that enabled Biden to stage an electoral "coup."

GEORGIA. Biden leads in Georgia by 14,000 votes. Georgia is headed to an automatic recount.

Republican Senators Kelly Loeffler and David Perdue, both in a hotly contested runoff to save their seats, have called for Secretary of State

Brad Raffensperger, another Republican, to resign because of his "failure" managing the election. "The voters of Georgia hired me, and the voters will be the one to fire me," Raffensperger shot back. "They ought to focus on their runoff."

WISCONSIN. Biden leads by 20,000 votes.

The morning after the election, Trump tweeted that his people were "finding Biden votes all over the place— in Pennsylvania, Wisconsin and Michigan." Giuliani elaborated on the charge that afternoon.

"In Wisconsin, mysteriously at 4 in the morning, 120,000 ballots appeared." Giuliani called it a "ballot dump" in Milwaukee County, a Democratic stronghold. "Here come these ballots. Well, we have no idea if they really are ballots."

They were. Around 3:30 a.m. the AP reported a 143,124 spike in Biden's Milwaukee County vote total, versus 23,642 for Trump. The results came from various tabulating sites in Milwaukee County, which, under Wisconsin law, reports all its returns in one lump sum. Election Commissioner Claire Woodall-Vogg said she would have given out partial returns earlier but wanted "to avoid this dramatic narrative that's completely false." Wisconsin is also headed to a recount.

NEVADA. Biden leads by 12,000 votes.

Trump's legal team put a new twist on frivolous lawsuits when they sent a letter to Attorney General William Barr asking him to investigate "criminal voter fraud" in Nevada.

"Nevada is turning out to be a cesspool of Fake Votes," Trump tweeted Monday, "absolutely shocking!"

The Nevada challenge is based on 3,000 voters who, according to an online change-of-address website, live out of state. Election officials say they are more likely military personnel on duty, out-of-state students, or recent arrivals.

PENNSYLVANIA. Biden leads by 47,000 votes. Giuliani has so muddied the waters with his gibberish lawsuits, there's not enough space here to explain all the state cases that judges have tossed out.

But Trump's last, spindly thread to the Supreme Court may be a challenge the Trump campaign filed before the election to a Pennsylvania law allowing election workers to count mail-in ballots received up to three days after the election.

The law was passed by the Republican-controlled legislature in the panic over the pandemic this summer and upheld by the Republican-controlled state Supreme Court. The U.S. Supreme Court twice refused to review the state court decision. But Justice Samuel Alito, hearing late-night emergency appeals, threw Republicans a lifeline.

Ballots postmarked before the election but received after Election Day had to be segregated off, Alito said, in case Republicans wanted to file a follow-up case. The 25,000 ballots at issue will not be enough to overcome Biden's lead.

Time is Running Out

If any of the Trump legal team's other lawsuits wind their way up to the Supreme Court, it's unlikely the justices will consider them before Dec. 8, the last day states have to certify their results. And the Electoral College meets six days later on Dec. 14 to cast the official votes.

This gives the Trump legal team 27 days to wade through the cesspool in Nevada, test the Sharpies in Arizona, kick around the ballot dumps in Wisconsin, and tell the politicians in Georgia to shut up and run. Then they have to come up with some new evidence of the "widespread vote fraud" they allege. Then prove it. Then show why it makes a difference.

I don't think democracy can wait for that. This isn't Bush v. Gore.

This is Donald Trump throwing a hissy fit.

— November 11, 2020

Donald J. Trump ✔ @realDonaldTrump · Nov 12

"REPORT: DOMINION DELETED 2.7 MILLION TRUMP VOTES
NATIONWIDE. DATA ANALYSIS FINDS 221,000 PENNSYLVANIA VOTES
SWITCHED FROM PRESIDENT TRUMP TO BIDEN. 941,000 TRUMP VOTES
DELETED. STATES USING DOMINION VOTING SYSTEMS SWITCHED
435,000 VOTES FROM TRUMP TO BIDEN." @ChanelRion @OANN

⚠ This claim about election fraud is disputed

The Big Kahuna
of Lies

IF DONALD TRUMP IS SO EAGER TO GET TO COURT, all he has to
do is step out of the White House on Jan. 21 where a line of process servers
will be waiting to serve him.

The first subpoena will come from E. Jean Carroll, the *Elle* magazine
advice columnist who says Trump sexually assaulted her in the dressing
room at Bergdorf Goodman in the mid-1990s. When she recounted the
incident in her 2019 book, the president took to Twitter to deny it. "She's
not my type," he scoffed.

Carroll has a defamation suit moving forward in a New York court
based on the tweet. Attorney General William Barr tried to get it transferred to federal court (to take advantage of presidential immunity), but a
federal judge kicked it back. Now that Trump is out of office, she can move

forward with her request for a sample of Trump's DNA to match a semen stain on the dress she was wearing. Sound familiar?

Next up may be Summer Zervos, a former *Apprentice* contestant, who claims Trump assaulted her in 2007 at the Beverly Hills Hotel. On Twitter, Trump denied the incident ever happened. She, too, has an active case against him for defamation.

And what about the other 24 women who claim Trump sexually assaulted them on airplanes, in bars, in pageant dressing rooms and hotels going back to the 1970s? A lot those claims have exceeded their legal expiration date, but the lurid details in the women's accounts make it clear that when Trump told Billy Bush on the *Access Hollywood* bus "You grab them by the pussy," he was the grabber in chief.

Then there are the contractors he stiffed building of the Trump International Hotel in Washington. According to *USA Today*, Trump and the Trump Organization were involved in 3,500 lawsuits for nonpayment of bills or wages over the three decades leading up to his presidency. So all you carpenters, painters, dishwashers, bartenders, lawyers and other contractors that Trump stiffed while he was in office, get in line.

Taxes

And don't forget the investigations into Trump's taxes by the New York attorney general and Manhattan District Attorney Cyrus Vance Jr. They won't have to stand in line. They already have subpoenas and a Supreme Court order. Vance wants a grand jury to see Trump's tax returns to determine whether he doctored his financial reporting to cover up hush-money payments to Stormy Daniels.

Should his taxes become public, they will likely become a part of another suit his niece Mary Trump has filed against him. It charges that Trump connived to cheat her out of her fair share of the estate passed on by his father, Fred.

And while we have his taxes on the table, why don't we have the IRS make him cough up the $72 million he owes from the disputed audit? That was the excuse he used to not release his returns in 2016. So let's get that pesky little dodge out of the way before he runs again in 2024.

The Big Kahuna of Lies

Then let's go after the Big Kahuna of Trump lies, the one he tweeted out Thursday charging that Dominion Voting Systems deleted 2.7 million Trump votes and switched 435,000 votes from Trump to Biden, thus stealing the election from him.

With his attempts to overturn the election flagging in the courts, the president has been casting around for any excuse to explain why Joe Biden, of all people, beat him, and Dominion Voting Systems was the perfect bogeyman.

Dominion was founded in 2001 by two Canadians after the "hanging chad" debacle in Florida. Voting officials all over America were demanding more high-tech options, and Dominion pushed to be a leader in the field. The company snapped up touch screens, scanners and counting software from industry leaders Diebold and ES&S, then started developing its own.

Today, it is the second largest supplier of voting software in America, with aspirations to be first. Its voting systems are used in 28 states and around the world. The voting systems serve 1,600 jurisdictions and handle 70 million votes a year.

So no one had more to lose when Trump tweeted out that Dominion software was the secret weapon in a conspiracy to steal his election. Its honesty, its reputation, its everything—and billions of dollars in lost revenue—hinge on whether Trump is right, or wrong.

Why would the president maliciously tweet out that Dominion software cost him 3 million votes? Where did Trump get that hare-brained idea?

The Michigan Glitch

As it turns out, on Election Day, in the mitten fingers of Michigan, in tiny Antrim County (pop. 23,580), there was a glitch in the system.

The voting had gone as usual, slow but steady, so the poll workers were surprised when they tallied up the ballots and found Joe Biden won by 3,000 votes in a county that normally goes Republican. They called in their tech guy—everybody has a tech guy—and he discovered two incompatible versions of the Dominion software had been loaded into the machines. The

209

problem was fixed. The tally was rerun and, sure enough, Trump won the county by 2,000 votes.

Meanwhile in Georgia, which bought $107 million of Dominion election gear last year, some of the poll workers were also struggling with the new Dominion software. In Gwinnett County, a suburb outside Atlanta, the votes were getting counted correctly, but the machines wouldn't transmit the tallies to the state's central database. That problem too was rectified, and the proper votes were registered.

But by then, it was too late.

Giuliani, On the Case

The Trump legal beagles were on the case. Rudy Giuliani, head of Trump's legal team, already had hundreds of lawyers out looking for vote fraud. His people were nosing around other Michigan counties that used Dominion machines, peering through paper-covered windows at the vote counting center in Detroit, and looking for missing Trump votes in Rochester Hills.

In his postelection press conference Thursday—the one where he said Big Media, Big Money and Big Tech were stealing the election from him—Trump said his legal team found all kinds of voting irregularities in Pennsylvania, Georgia and North Carolina. On Friday, RNC Chair Ronna McDaniel held her own press conference in Michigan to support him.

She said Republicans had found thousands of missing Trump votes in Antrim and identified 47 other Michigan counties that used Dominion software. She wanted all of them recounted by hand. On Sean Hannity's show that night, Trump's personal attorney Jay Sekulow said *he* wanted a manual recount in every county, anywhere, that used the Dominion machines.

"If 30 states have used software where there's already proved to be a glitch of 6,000 votes in, lawyers for the campaign should, in every one of those jurisdictions, demand a fix and a manual recount," he said.

A Vast Right-Wing Conspiracy

The mainstream media buried the Antrim glitch in an array of vote fraud claims the Trump camp was making. But on 8kun, a website often thought to be a gathering point for QAnon conspiracy buffs, an anonymous poster claimed it was only the tip of the iceberg of computer vote fraud.

Within hours, 8kun's post was careening around the right wing of the internet (from Reddit to Parler to Twitter to Chance) like the secret codes for Call of Duty. Bloggers from all parts of the country were posting up personal testimony to other Dominion election machine malfunctions, or rumors of them, past and present.

The Trump team set up an 800 line to collect voter fraud complaints (but had to take it down because it was getting too many crank calls.) Over the weekend, *The New York Times* reported there were more than 3,700 posts on Facebook mentioning "election," "software" and "glitch" that were collectively shared more than 250,000 times.

On Sunday morning *Blabber Buzz*, a mouthpiece for *Gateway Pundit* Joe Hoft, sent out an email alert. "Corrupted Software Which Gave Biden Michigan Win Also Used in These States." An hour later, *Breitbart News* followed with a story headlined "Researchers Question Reliability of Dominion Voting Systems, Election Systems & Software." It appears that at a recent DefCon convention in Las Vegas, a hacker was able to crack two older ballot-marking devices similar to Dominion's. And it only took eight hours.

On Tuesday night, the *Gateway Pundit* published another blockbuster. BREAKING EXCLUSIVE: Analysis of Election Night Data from All States Shows MILLIONS of VOTES Either Switched from President Trump or Were Lost—Using Dominion and Other Systems.

That story pointed to a blogger named thedonald.win who had worked out a mathematical model showing Trump had 2,737,939 votes deleted, and 451,517 switched from Trump to Biden in voting districts that used Dominion Voting Systems. Hoft said he could not verify it. I looked at it. I didn't see any math errors. But so what? It's just a piece of the puzzle, Hoft said. "It looks like the Democrats did everything imaginable in their attempt to steal the election. The problem was that they never expected President Trump to lead a record-breaking campaign, and they got caught."

The online buzz about Dominion caught the attention of Kayleigh McEnany, but Trump didn't mention it on Twitter until he saw Lou Dobbs a couple nights later on Fox. "I don't care what state you are in, this computer voting is wide open to fraud and intervention," Dobb opined. To which Trump tweeted, "True, and wait until you see what's coming."

I Alone Has a Day of Reckoning

Trump spent three days fending off demands he concede, getting encouraging reports from Giuliani, and brooding that the media wasn't paying any attention. He had people filing lawsuits in five states, and all the media reported on were the ones getting tossed.

Chanel Rion, the White House correspondent for the One America News, was walking around the White House Tuesday night and bumped into the president. She's one of his favorite reporters. She's the one he always calls on for the last softball question.

She told him about her story (natch!) on OAN about Dominion system software glitches, with Rudy as her guest expert, then she asked if he'd seen the latest *Gateway Pundit*. The pundit had numbers on how many votes the Democrats stole, she said, and Trump would drop his drawers (not that it takes much) when he saw how many votes Dominion's computer glitch cost him: 2.7 million.

On Wednesday, Giuliani elaborated on the charges at a press conference. He explained how computer voting software works. Briefly, since he doesn't have the slightest idea. Then he went on to tell reporters his team was finding "voter irregularities" all over Pennsylvania, and he had a "whistleblower" inside Dominion who was guiding his team to more.

Finally, Trump had a simple, unifying theme that explained why he lost to Biden. The voting machines were rigged.

I don't have the presidential schedule for Wednesday, but Trump must have had a lot of voices swirling around in his head from friends telling him what to do. The ones he was listening to gravitated around this claim that he lost because the computers were rigged. Dobbs, Giuliani, Rion, McEnany, and, no doubt, his sons were on board. And now *Gateway Pundit* had the numbers to prove it.

In that stew of a mind he gets into late at night, he knew what he wanted to say. He woke up Thursday morning, hit the ALL CAPS button, and let loose.

 Donald J. Trump ✔ @realDonaldTrump · Nov 12

"REPORT: DOMINION DELETED 2.7 MILLION TRUMP VOTES NATIONWIDE. DATA ANALYSIS FINDS 221,000 PENNSYLVANIA VOTES SWITCHED FROM PRESIDENT TRUMP TO BIDEN. 941,000 TRUMP VOTES DELETED. STATES USING DOMINION VOTING SYSTEMS SWITCHED 435,000 VOTES FROM TRUMP TO BIDEN." @ChanelRion @OANN

⚠ This claim about election fraud is disputed

Thursday afternoon, Dominion shot back. "Claims about Dominion switching or deleting votes are 100 percent false," it said in a detailed response. So too are allegations about software updates being done the night before an election. And Trump's math is preposterous.

"Claims that 2.7 million votes for President Trump were deleted— including 941,000 in Pennsylvania—are mathematically impossible. In Pennsylvania, Dominion serves 14 counties that produced 1.3 million votes with a voter turnout of 76 percent. Fifty-two percent of those votes went to President Trump. Calculating that out, Dominion processed about 676,000 votes for the President in Pennsylvania. There never were 941,000 votes to 'delete.'"

Bankrupt Him!

So Donald Trump's presidency will end the same way it began. On the down escalator to a rabbit hole filled with the darkest, most malicious, and most ridiculous lies he's ever told.

If I were running Dominion Voting Systems, I'd sue him for every dime he has. Take the deed to Mar-a-Lago. Turn his golf courses into wind farms. Bankrupt him.

This wasn't the protected speech of a president. For that, he had Whitehouse.gov. This was a crazed politician using the megaphone of his bully pulpit to spread a venomous lie and poison the global market for your product. The damages to your reputation, and revenues, are incalculable.

Plus, there's a bonus in holding Trump's trial in a civil courtroom. In every libel case, the fulcrum of truth is center stage, and Trump's fate will hang in the balance. Doesn't that sound great?

LIBEL COURT.

We can make it into a game show. Trump can be the host.

But seriously, the only truth *this* fulcrum will be deciding is:

Was Donald Trump lying? And how much will it cost him?

We don't have to wrangle over whether Democrats stole the election. We don't need a recount. We don't need the Supreme Court. Wait until Jan. 21.

Let's have a jury of Donald Trump's peers decide, once and for all, whether the 2020 election was free and fair.

— November 15, 2020

LOSER

LET'S TRY THIS AGAIN. Donald Trump lost the 2020 election to Joe Biden. Decisively. By a wide margin. In a free and fair election.

Donald, can you step to the front of the class and say it? I am a loser. Yes, it is humiliating to have to admit it. But we can only have one teacher at a time in this class, and until you say it there are students here who will go to their grave believing America chooses its leaders based on who has the most Twitter followers, not who got the most votes.

On Monday, the Electoral College, a quaint institution set up by your favorite Founding Fathers, will confirm that Joe Biden received 81,282,903 votes, and Donald Trump got 74,223,030. They were cast, in person or by mail, at tens of thousands of polling places across America.

Republican and Democratic volunteers came together, as they do every election, to make sure the election machinery ran smoothly. That was especially hard this year because of the coronavirus pandemic. Many longtime poll workers didn't volunteer for fear of contracting the virus, and a majority of voters chose to send in absentee ballots for the same reason. The counting took longer than expected, but state and county election officials anticipated the problem and set up safeguards to make sure every vote was counted. Poll workers didn't complain about the laborious process, even as your designated "poll watchers" peeked over their shoulders and shot videos of them through the windows.

Christopher Krebs, the director of cybersecurity you appointed to safeguard the election process, called it "the most secure election in American history."

The state-by-state totals gave Biden 306 Electoral College votes to your 232, the same margin that you called a landslide four years ago. In five states, at the insistence of Republicans, the votes were recounted (three times in Georgia). The results did not change.

On election night, you started a drumbeat that led us to the current moment. At 2:30 in the morning, to the accompaniment of "Hail to the Chief," you stepped to the microphone to declare yourself the winner and decree that all voting must stop. You were proud of the states where you appeared to be winning or held big leads. Then you said, "All of a sudden everything stopped. This is a fraud on the American republic, this is an embarrassment to our country."

When you declared your victory, only 85% of the votes had been counted—7 million fewer than the 2016 vote total and 23 million votes short of the ultimate tally. But you couldn't get it out of your head that the Democrats "stole" your election. So you spent the rest of the night riffing on Twitter (22 times) about secret late-night ballot dumps, rigged machines, dead people voting, switched votes, deleted votes, and a nefarious Democratic plot to steal your victory.

In your mind, the narrative was set. The next day your crack legal team, led by Rudy Giuliani and Jenna Ellis, set about trying to prove it. They filed 60 lawsuits in 60 different state courts, and 59 of them were dismissed for lack of evidence. Finally, as the last state legislatures certified Biden's win Tuesday, the Supreme Court refused (unanimously) to consider a desperate challenge to the Pennsylvania voting law that the Pennsylvania Supreme Court had already upheld.

In the weeks following the election, you have obsessed over your defeat, to the exclusion of anything else. If 75 people walked into your Oval Office, *The Washington Post*'s Ashley Parker reported, they got 75 versions of the same rant. You were robbed. In a summit called to celebrate your COVID-19 vaccines, you managed to take the conversation around to who has the guts to toss out the election results.

"Let's see whether or not somebody has the courage, whether it's a legislator or legislatures, or whether it's a Justice of the Supreme Court or a number of Justices of the Supreme Court, let's see if they have the courage to do what everybody in this country knows is right."

Your despair over your loss is understandable. You ran a terrific campaign by modern-day standards. You raised and spent over $1 billion, mostly on the internet, before the campaign even began. Your rallies generated millions of email addresses that were fed into a sophisticated database your campaign used to target supporters by states, counties and 100 other criteria. The highest rated cable channel, Fox News, was a perpetual propaganda machine for you. Sean Hannity, Tucker Carlson, Lou Dobbs and Laura Ingraham carried water for you every night. And you garnered 74 million votes—12 million more than you got in 2016.

Unfortunately, Joe Biden got 81 million. Their votes went to a man campaigning in a mask from his basement on the promise he would bring an end to the *sturm und drang* of the Trump years. "Will you shut up, man!" he said, and in that phrase, he captured the mood of the nation.

So Donald, accept it. You lost. Now please step to the chalkboard and write 100 times *I'm a loser, I'm a loser, I'm a loser, I'm a loser, I'm a loser, I'm a loser, I'm a loser, I'm a loser, I'm a loser, I'm a loser…*

And never forget it.

— December 9, 2020

The End is Near

Biden Masks

ON THE SATURDAY JOE BIDEN WAS DECLARED THE WINNER of the November election, my neighbors gathered outside on the sidewalk celebrating, as they usually do, with a cocktail. Since the COVID-19 crisis began, this is what passes for a social occasion on our block because all the bars, restaurants and entertainment venues are still closed.

Over the summer, we gathered there almost every evening, our kids running in and out of houses, dogs lapping at our feet. One neighbor, a laid-off chef, brought appetizers. Others brought work they were doing from home. And we were all maskless since, as they say in school, we were with our cohort. We spent so much time together we thought we were immune. Everything was okay because we never left our block. Until it wasn't. Patrick tested positive.

When I joined them, they were all wearing masks. "These are our Biden masks," my neighbor said. "We all just want this whole thing to be over."

A second wave of the coronavirus has indeed swelled. On Election Day, 100,000 new cases of coronavirus were diagnosed in America. Two weeks later, that number was up to 150,000, and it's not because we are testing more, as Trump claimed throughout the campaign. The hospitals are bursting at the seams. The death toll is over 250,000. Doctors and nurses are exhausted. Nobody feels safe anymore, cohort or not. Somebody had to do something.

Enter Joe Biden

Enter Joe Biden. The network news these days alternately opens with grim scenes from hospital ICUs or the foolishness of Trump lawyers going to court to challenge the election returns. Thank God Biden has kept his eye on the ball. His first meeting after his election was with his coronavirus task force, a loose confederation of immunologists, infectious disease doctors and public health experts, including Rick Bright, the former head of vaccine research Trump fired in May. They are working out a plan to confront the spread of the virus, and I somehow have confidence it will work because they've been working on it quietly for months.

They will take office on the fortuitous news that not one, but two vaccines are out of clinical trials, and both are 95% effective. These are the vaccines Trump was counting on to pull him out of his political trough before Election Day. But they come with a serious dose of seriousness, the Biden team warned.

Even under an emergency order, the first batch will not be available until the end of the year, and it's likely the drug manufacturers will not be able to manufacture more than 20 million doses a month. The first batch will go to doctors, nurses, teachers, police, fire fighters, and so on down a list of essential workers. The general public will not see them until April or May.

President Trump has boasted that he has the whole U.S. Army mobilized to distribute them. As soon as the FDA gives the go-ahead, he seems to think Army trucks are going to pull up to the loading dock, drive the vaccines out to every little village and town, and throw them off the back like they are tossing out paper towels in Puerto Rico.

But it's not that easy. One of the vaccines has to be transported in refrigerated cases set at 94 degrees below zero. Both require two doses, a primary and a booster, so doctors will have to maintain records on who got what when. And the whole task won't be completed until there are shots in the arms of 330 million Americans.

The complexity of the problem is one reason the Biden team is frustrated by the president's refusal to open lines of communication with his coronavirus team during the transition. A slip-up anywhere along the line can push back distribution a month, or two, or maybe never if people are so freaked by the president's pronouncements that they won't take it.

'I Take No Responsibility'

For President Trump, this whole coronavirus thing is China's fault. (It's always someone else's fault.) If China had contained the virus to Wuhan last December, none of this would be happening. Then it was the Democrats' fault. The outbreaks were only happening in blue states run by incompetent Democratic governors. Then it was a "deep state conspiracy" at the Centers for Disease Control and Prevention and the FDA to hold off releasing vaccines until after Election Day—to make Trump look bad.

For Trump, it was always about his reelection. At first, he warmed to the idea he had a Coronavirus Task Force working on the problem. He didn't have the slightest idea what that entailed. But their daily press conference was doing gangbuster numbers, so he decided to horn in. "It's like a really bad flu, right?" he'd ask or "Can't you inject some kind of bleach to kill it?" Even he could see that wasn't working.

Trump balked when the task force told him in March he had to shut down "the greatest economy in the history of the world." At that point, there were 500,000 diagnosed cases in America, and 20,000 deaths. His first thought was to "reopen" on Easter (April 12) so people could go to church and thank God it's over.

When his task force pushed the shutdown out to April 30, with a phased reopening based on certain metrics, he encouraged some Republican governors to ignore them. "We can't let the cure be worse than the problem," he said. By the middle of June, he was tired of this whole mitigation strategy.

He stopped attending Coronavirus Task Force meetings. If anything important happened, he trusted Mike Pence to tell him. He openly challenged Dr. Fauci. "He's got this high approval rating. So why don't I have a high approval rating?" he asked. Then he replaced Fauci at his press conferences with Dr. Scott Atlas, a radiologist who doubles as a Fox news contributor.

The Maskless Campaign

Trump wanted to get back on the campaign trail. He'd taken heat from the press for not wearing a mask, but on the campaign trail, strutting around stage without a mask, he could see his supporters loved him for it.

"Wearing a mask is an individual decision," he told them. They roared their approval. (You can't roar if you are wearing a mask.) They stood together observing enough social distance not to step on each other's toes and feeding off his confidence. The worst is over, Trump promised them.

"We are rounding the corner.... There will be a vaccine before the end of the year.... We're doing great. Our numbers are incredible...I think we've probably done the best job of any country.... If you take the blue states out, we're at a level I don't think anybody in the world would be at."

He returned to his regime of campaign rallies Aug. 17 in Oshkosh. At that point, 5 million Americans were infected by the disease, and the death toll was 170,000. Trump relished the idea he was out with the people while Sleepy Joe was campaigning from his basement.

He mocked Biden for wearing a mask. "I don't wear a mask like him," he said. "Every time you see him, he's got a mask. He could be speaking 200 feet away and he shows up with the biggest mask I've ever seen."

The mask was a symbol of his defiance and the fortitude of his supporters. It became the leading indicator of which side of the Great Divide in America you were on. Do you want to get the economy moving again, or do you want to make America healthy again? Biden's response was that you couldn't get the economy moving until you vanquished the virus.

Trump flouted his defiance right up to the first presidential debate, where his recklessness came crashing down on him. He skipped the mandatory COVID test (and maybe a few others before at the White House) and came down with COVID himself.

The Superspreader

It's likely he picked up the virus three days earlier at a White House ceremony for his new Supreme Court nominee Amy Coney Barrett. About 300 prominent Republicans attended. The White House did a perfunctory rapid-response COVID test as they entered, so only a few wore masks.

The following week, it became clear the White House was a cesspool of viral germs. Hope Hicks, Trump's longtime personal assistant, was the first to test positive. Then Kellyanne Conway, Ronna McDaniel, Kayleigh McEnany, Chris Christie, Senators Mike Lee of Utah and Thom Tillis from North Carolina, Robert O'Brien, the national security adviser who first warned of the virus, Melania Trump, and their son Barron. There were others whose names were not released. Trump's valet, his congressional liaison, the Marine who carries the football with the nuclear codes, three White House reporters. Some 130 Secret Service agents who had been out on the campaign trail with the president were put in quarantine.

When Trump's condition worsened, he was taken to Walter Reed hospital where a team of doctors administered a mix of experimental drugs. Two days later, he emerged for another photo-op staged during the nightly network newscasts. A helicopter set down on the White House lawn. Trump walked up to the steps to the Truman Balcony, paused, and ripped the mask off his face.

Then he did a second take for the TV commercial.

Give Me a Break

As I walk around Chicago after the election, there's a sense of relief that Trump is gone, or almost gone, or will be dragged out of the White House by his heels if he doesn't leave.

The coronavirus is raging. Twelve million people are now infected, over 250,000 dead, and hospitals once again are over-stuffed with patients.

The president hasn't appeared in public in 12 days. He's consumed in this doomed mission to prove the election was stolen. But at least we can be grateful he's not sputtering nonsense about turning the corner or promising a rubber band rebound in the economy. We need some respite from that. We're exhausted. A strong dose of reality, not the television kind, is just what the doctor ordered.

— November 20, 2020

'Tis the Season to Be Bad

IT LOOKS TO ME LIKE SANTA came down the chimney early at the White House this week and dumped his naughty list on President Trump's desk for reconsideration.

The president started handing out pardons and commutations a couple days before Christmas. Twenty in all, three for disgraced congressmen, two for minor functionaries caught up in the Russia investigation, four for Blackwater mercenaries who killed 17 Iraqi civilians in a town square, two for border patrol agents who shot an unarmed immigrant, one for a Utah county commissioner caught driving an ATV on government land, and another for a moonshiner caught in a 1952 raid on his still.

OK, I'll give you the moonshiner. He's not likely to go back to his wicked ways. And anybody can lose their way on an ATV in the desert. But the congressmen? All big Trump supporters, of course. What did they do?

All Rep. Chris Collins did was pull out his cellphone at a White House picnic to tip his son to a failed FDA drug trial that would adversely affect his biotech company. The son, in turn, used that inside information to sell company stock and avoid a $750,000 loss. But isn't that par for the course? Certainly no worse than the stock sales Senators David Perdue and Kelly Loeffler made earlier this year after getting briefed on the coronavirus, and they're both running for reelection in the Georgia special election.

Reps. Duncan Hunter of California and Steve Stockman of Texas engaged in the more garden-variety form of corruption. Duncan took over $200,000 from his campaign funds and spent it on an extramarital affair, overseas vacations, private school for his children and plane tickets for his pet rabbits. Stockman was serving out a 10-year sentence for a white-collar crime spree that included 23 felony counts of fraud and laundering $1.1million of campaign funds.

But Trump was just warming up. The next day, he issued 26 more pardons. The marquee names were Paul Manafort and Roger Stone, once partners in a Washington political consulting firm, who both went to jail after stonewalling investigators in the Mueller Russia probe. And Charles Kushner, Jared's father, also made the list after serving 14 months for tax evasion and witness tampering.

The Pardon Process

The granting of pardons is one of the more loosey-goosey powers of the presidency. Alexander Hamilton put it in the Constitution as a way for the government to show mercy or correct injustices, but presidents have wide latitude granting clemency and usually take full advantage at the end of their term.

There is an Office of the Pardon Attorney in the Justice Department that has a budget of $4.5 million and 19 employees to sift through the current 14,000 pardon applications. Trump has largely gone around them to reward allies and supporters. Other presidents have stirred controversy with their pardons. Bill Clinton used his pardon power to erase his brother Roger's drug conviction. George H.W. Bush exonerated his former Secretary of Defense Caspar Weinberger and four others involved in the Reagan-era Iran-Contra affair. And Clinton's controversial pardon of fugitive international trader Marc Rich, whose ex-wife was a major contributor to Hillary's Senate campaign and the Clinton Foundation, prompted a congressional investigation after he left office.

But Donald Trump has taken the pardon process to a whole new level, and it's far from over. Will Rudy Giuliani get a pardon for bad lawyering? Can Saudi Arabian Prince Mohammed bin Salman get a pardon for chopping up a *Washington Post* columnist with a bone saw? Will Trump give a blanket pardon to his sons, Don Jr. and Eric, his daughter Ivanka and husband Jared for crimes yet to be charged? Will he pardon himself? Is that even possible?

Manafort and Stone

The pardons for Manafort and Stone are signs of how much Trump values loyalty. Both were central figures in the Russia investigation, and both were found guilty of lying to authorities about what they knew. Stone once boasted of his close relationship to WikiLeaks head Julian Assange, then dodged congressional inquiries into his role in Assange's release of Democratic emails two hours after the *Access Hollywood* tapes surfaced.

Manafort was serving a seven-year sentence for tax charges related to his political work in Ukraine. At one point, he cut a deal with prosecutors to testify about potential Trump campaign connections to Russia in exchange for leniency; then he tried to co-ordinate his testimony with Trump's lawyers, and the deal fell apart.

During the Mueller probe, the White House used every legal argument in its arsenal to protect the president. Subpoenas, documents and interview requests were routinely rejected as a violation of presidential prerogatives. When Mueller finally got the president to agree to an interview, his lawyers would only allow written questions, and Trump did not answer half of them.

The Code of Silence

In his report, Mueller cited 10 incidents that might constitute obstruction of justice but left it to Congress to pursue charges because of a Justice Department rule against indicting sitting presidents. Andrew Weissmann, a senior prosecutor for Mueller, calls the pardons for Stone and Manafort "the final act" in Trump's obstruction of justice.

"The pardons from this president are what you would expect to get if you gave the pardon power to a mob boss," he said. They're a reward for not ratting him out.

"President Trump doesn't use his pardon power often, but when he does, he abuses the process for all it's worth," *The New York Times* wrote in a Christmas Eve editorial. "Mr. Trump's stingy, self-serving approach to clemency is due in part to his transactional view of the law as something to be used to punish his enemies and to protect himself, his friends and his allies. But it's a power that is easy to abuse because it is nearly unlimited."

The King of Medicaid Fraud

One of the most puzzling of the Trump commutations went to Philip Esformes, the owner of a string of nursing homes that swindled Medicare and Medicaid out of $1.3 billion.

Last year, a federal judge in Miami sentenced Esformes to 20 years in jail for cycling elderly, destitute and drug-addicted patients through his network of 20 facilities. He billed millions of dollars in fraudulent claims to Medicare and other government programs every year, often for services never rendered. The judge called the scheme an epic violation of trust "unmatched in our community, if not the country."

Trump's commutation means Esformes will serve less than a year of his 20-year sentence. His clemency was sponsored by the Aleph Institute, an organization founded by the Chabad-Lubavitch sect of Hassidic Jews. Jared Kushner attends services at a Chabad temple near his home in Washington, and advocates for Esformes include Alan Dershowitz and Ken Starr, attorneys for Trump during his impeachment, who are affiliated with the institute.

White House Press Secretary Kayleigh McEnany justified the clemency on the grounds that Esformes, who is 52, suffers from declining health and "has been devoted to prayer and repentance."

Before he got sick and found God, the *Chicago Tribune* reported Esformes would fly around the country in private jets between mansions he owns in Los Angeles and Miami and a luxury condominium on Michigan Avenue. He drives a $1.6 million Ferrari Aperta, once chauffeured prostitutes to Orlando for a tryst at the Ritz-Carlton Hotel and paid $300,000 to the men's basketball coach at the University of Pennsylvania to get his son into school there.

Some 90% of the pardons Trump has issued so far have gone to friends of his allies or campaign donors, according to *The New York Times*. And the holidays have just begun. Over the next three weeks, I'm sure there will be more.

Donald Trump is going to pardon anyone he wants, for whatever reason he wants, because he can. And they can all celebrate afterwards over dinner on the patio in Mar-a-Lago.

— December 26, 2020

An Avalanche of Chaos, Corruption and Confusion

WHILE THE PRESIDENT GOLFED and Vice President Mike Pence was skiing in Vail, the $900 billion COVID relief package sat unsigned on President Trump's desk. Twelve million Americans lost their unemployment insurance, millions more face eviction by the end of the week, COVID-19 infections in America topped 19 million, hospital ICUs were at capacity, the government was on the brink of a shutdown…and President Trump tweeted:

"Courts are bad, the FBI and 'Justice' didn't do their job, and the United States Election System looks like that of a third world country. But when it is all over, and this period of time becomes just another ugly chapter in our Country's history, WE WILL WIN!!"

"This president is leaving office in an avalanche of chaos, corruption and confusion," John Garamendi, a Democratic congressman from the Sacramento Valley, told MSNBC.

"I don't understand what's being done, or why, unless it's just to create chaos and show power and be upset because you lost the election," Adam Kinzinger, a Republican representative from Rockford, scolded on CNN.

And then Rupert Murdoch, the man at the top of the Fox News empire, and a stanch Trump ally, weighed in on the front page of his *New York Post*.

"Mr. President, it's time to end this dark charade," the *Post* wrote in a Sunday editorial. "You had every right to investigate the election. But let's be clear: Those efforts have found nothing. We understand, Mr. President, that you're angry that you lost. But to continue down this road is ruinous."

Trump's Last Stand

In the final hours of the weekend, Trump finally did sign the COVID-19 relief bill and a budget authorization to avoid a government shutdown. But he is as committed as ever to making the Jan. 6 session of Congress—where they will receive the Electoral College vote—his last stand. So he is twisting the arm of every Republican he can to vote against accepting the Electoral College results—and calling for his legion of followers to demonstrate outside.

For Garamendi, Trump's last stand ends fittingly with a lie. "Let's go back to the very first day the president was inaugurated," Garamendi said. "He lied about the size of the crowd, and he's lied every day since. He holds to nothing. Whatever comes to his mind at that moment is where he is. And that's the confusion and the chaos that he has sown into this entire four years. The fact of the matter is you can't believe anything the president says, or tweets, or writes."

Health Care

Take health care. The mantra of Republicans since Obamacare was passed 10 years ago has been "repeal and replace." During the 2016 campaign, Trump went around the country saying repeal was going to be easy. At various times, he called his various health care plans "terrific, "fantastic" and "phenomenal." But none of them ever made it onto paper.

The closest he came was in his first year when he held a celebration at the White House for a House bill he called "incredibly well-crafted." A week later, he denounced it as "mean" when he tried to get it through the Senate. He throttled down funds for Obamacare enrollment, repealed the individual mandate and nibbled at the edges of "wasteful" health care spending, but offered no alternative.

The Economy

You have to be living under a rock not to know Donald Trump presided over "the greatest economy in the history of the world." Or so he says.

But how much credit does he deserve? (My brother, a disciple of Milton Friedman, says not much because today's global economy responds more to market forces than government interference.)

Let's acknowledge the U.S. economy was running on all cylinders before the coronavirus shut it down in March. The Dow Jones index was bobbing around 29,000 in February. Unemployment was 3.5%, a record low, and Trump boasted that 160 million Americans had jobs. "More Americans are working by far than ever before." But how much of that is due to Trump, and how much to population growth? During the Great Depression, 160 million people couldn't go back to work because there were only 130 million people in the whole country.

And for seven of the 10 years that the economy was rising, Barack Obama was the presiding officer. Monthly job growth in Obama's last term was higher than in Trump's first, and annual deficits left over from the Wall Street bailout in 2008 were shrinking.

Trump's contribution to the economy came largely from a tax reform package House Speaker Paul Ryan put together that took effect in January 2018. For years, Ryan had championed a tax reform package that would lower the corporate tax rate from 35% to 28% and offset revenue losses by closing tax loopholes. His aim was a revenue neutral simplification of the tax code.

In Trump's hands, Ryan's balanced approach quickly became the "Cuts, Cuts, Cuts Act." Trump insisted the corporate rate drop to an unrealistic 21%, and most of the loopholes remained open (especially for real estate). Republicans sprinkled a bunch of little tax benefits around for the middle class—like a higher standard deduction, expanded family tax credits, and realigned tax brackets. They amounted to an extra $390 to $930 for families earning under $150,000, but taxpayers earning over $732,000 (the wealthiest 1%) received an average $51,400 in tax savings.

And the Cuts, Cuts, Cuts Act was anything but revenue neutral. It blew a $1 trillion hole in the annual federal budget, fueling a surge in consumer spending. The anticipated new tax revenue from corporate reinvestment never materialized; so the national debt, which was $20 trillion when Trump took office, is $27.75 trillion as he leaves.

Immigration

"I will build a great wall," Donald Trump promised. "I will build a great, great wall on our southern border, and I will make Mexico pay for that wall. Mark my words."

Nothing says Donald Trump like a wall—"an impenetrable, physical, tall, powerful, beautiful, southern border wall"—to stem the tide of illegal immigrants flowing into America.

Sometimes he said it was going to run sea-to-shining sea (1,954 miles). That it was going to be 60 feet high, with cameras and sensors to stop tunneling below and helicopters hovering above. His descriptions were fluid. It was going to be whatever popped into his mind at his rallies because it was all a mirage, a figment of his imagination.

In his four years in office, President Trump begged, borrowed or stole $15 billion from various federal budgets to build his wall. He shut down the government to get money out of Congress, declared a national emergency, trekked to the Supreme Court to release $2.5 billion from the Defense Department budget, and never got a dime out of Mexico.

What does he have to show for it? Some 423 miles of new wall, all but nine miles of it built to replace crumbling old barriers constructed decades ago. Forget what a boondoggle this has been for the world's greatest builder. The cost per mile of his wall is five times what it was during the Obama administration. Forget the human cost of separating children from their families, the strain on immigration courts, the fear his rhetoric spread through our immigrant communities.

What has his wall done to cut off illegal border crossings from Mexico? Under President Obama, Customs and Border Protection statistics show apprehensions of illegal immigrants along the southwestern border averaged 46,000 a month, versus 33,000 under Trump. This October and November, however, the latest CBP statistics show there were 70,000 illegal border crossings a month—about 5,000 *more* than under Obama in his last days in office.

The irony is that Trump had his greatest success cutting off illegal border crossings early in his term when the only weapon at his disposal was his mouth. (Only 20,000 people a month attempted to cross.) Maybe if we really want to secure our borders, we should put a bunch of stuffed Trump effigies along the border, like farmers put out scarecrows, with sound chips that say, "This is Donald Trump, and I'm still here." That will scare them off.

And So Forth

And don't forget our trade war with China. "Trade wars are good, and easy to win," Trump promised. But after three years of yo-yoing tariff hikes back and forth, our trade deficit with China is worse than when he started. Or his determination to put "America First" on the world stage where, after spending countless billions of dollars on military hardware, our prestige among world leaders is half what it was when he came into office. Or his promise to drain the swamp in Washington. Don't get me started.

All the problems Donald Trump so cavalierly promised to fix have been snowplowed down the road to this moment in time when a crisis—a real crisis he said would magically disappear like the flu—has revealed the breadth of his ignorance and the reckless course of his governance.

All we can do now is sit at the bottom of the hill in the logjam of his incompetence waiting for someone who knows what they are doing to pull us out.

— December 29, 2020

You Mean
It's Not Over?

A Constitutional Crisis, Trump Style

ONLY DONALD TRUMP COULD MAKE a constitutional crisis out of an eviction notice. When you lose an election by 7 million votes and 74 electors, you're in territory he once called a landslide. When you claim fraud in 60 different courtrooms in six different states, and 59 judges, Republicans and Democrats, say your case has no merit, that's a sign you should start packing. And when the Supreme Court, with three judges you appointed, says you have no standing to appeal, it's time to steal as much silverware as you can, and skedaddle.

But Donald Trump doesn't turn tail and run. He turns tail and blows farts in the face of democracy. If he can't win, he's going to cast a stench over the whole election process. He's going to browbeat every belly-sucking Republican he can into refusing to accept the vote of the Electoral College and let Mike Pence pick the next president. That, at least, was the fantasy going around in his head. He was going to give them something to remember him by.

No Time for Parties

The president had it all lined up for his Republican minions in Congress to contest Biden's victory when they met in joint session to count the Electoral College votes. Normally, this is a routine affair. The envelopes from each state are opened, the votes counted, and the tally is handed to the vice president to announce the winner. But Trump had 12 senators and 140 House Republicans ready to object because of the "voter irregularities" the president has been touting since election night, and legions of faithful MAGA heads he invited to Washington to gather outside Congress in protest.

"Be there," he tweeted. "Will be wild!"

He cut short his Mar-a-Lago vacation—skipping his famous New Year's Eve celebration with Vanilla Ice and the Beach Boys—to return to Washington to coordinate the attack. According to his official schedule, he would make no public appearances but "will make many calls and have many meetings" over the weekend, i.e., he won't be playing golf.

The Phone Call

One of them, unfortunately, was a Saturday call to the Republican secretary of state in Georgia, Brad Raffensperger. After six weeks of recounts and endless hours of court suits and hearings, Raffensperger was confident certifying that Joe Biden won Georgia by 11,779 votes. But Trump was sure he could persuade him to "recalculate."

Trump's Chief of Staff Mark Meadows and Peter Navarro, a longtime adviser whose *The Art of the Steal* was a cheat sheet for Trump grievances, were on the line, as was Raffensperger's general counsel, Ryan Germany, and a tape recorder.

For over an hour, Trump tried to bully, threaten and otherwise cajole Raffensperger into changing the Georgia count. Point by point, Raffensperger refuted him.

Trump claimed 5,000 dead people voted. Raffensperger said his office found only two instances of this. Trump claimed an election worker ran electronic ballots through a scanner three times to give Biden an extra 18,000 votes. Raffensperger said state investigators talked to the woman and recounted the ballots by hand. The tallies matched. Trump offered a statistical analysis that showed the rejection rate for absentee ballots was impossibly low. "I won Georgia," he kept repeating, probably by 500,000 votes.

"Well, Mr. President, the challenge that you have is the data you have is wrong," Raffensperger said.

Finally, an exasperated Trump got to his bottom line. "All I want to do is this. I just want to find 11,780 votes, which is one more than we have because we won the state."

The Tape

When the call ended, Raffensperger was ready to chalk it up to Trump being Trump. But the president wouldn't let it go.

On Sunday morning, Trump tweeted. "I spoke to Secretary of State Brad Raffensperger yesterday about Fulton County and voter fraud in Georgia. He was unwilling, or unable, to answer questions such as the 'ballots under the table' scam, ballot destruction, out of state 'voters,' dead voters, and more. He has no clue!"

"Respectfully, President Trump: What you're saying is not true," Raffensperger shot back. "The truth will come out." And it did.

The tape of the conversation appeared on the *Washington Post* website three hours later. In the cold type of a newspaper, Trump's threats looked dangerously close to vote tampering. But the tone of Trump's voice on the tape made him sound even more ominous, like a menacing, desperate president willing to do anything to preserve his fiefdom.

Clear Warnings

Sunday afternoon, wiser heads stepped in. From Wisconsin, former House Speaker Paul Ryan issued a statement castigating his former colleagues for going along with Trump's challenge.

"Efforts to reject the votes of the Electoral College and sow doubt about Joe Biden's victory strike at the foundation of our republic. It is difficult to conceive of a more anti-democratic and anti-conservative act than a federal intervention to overturn the results of state-certified elections and disenfranchise millions of Americans. The fact that this effort will fail does not mean it will not do significant damage to American democracy."

Ten former Secretaries of Defense—from Don Rumsfeld and Dick Cheney to James Mattis and the recently fired Mark Esper—signed an op-ed in *The Washington Post* warning that involving the military in the dispute would cross into "dangerous territory."

"Our elections have occurred. Recounts and audits have been conducted. Appropriate challenges have been addressed by the courts. Governors have certified the results. And the electoral college has voted. The time for questioning the results has passed; the time for the formal counting of the electoral college votes, as prescribed in the Constitution and statute, has arrived."

Senator Pat Toomey, a Republican from Pennsylvania, called Trump's phone call "a new low in this whole futile and sorry episode." Adam Kinzinger, the Republican congressman from Illinois, said in the wake of the call, no member of Congress could object to the election results with a "clean conscience."

The Last Rally

But Trump was unfazed. He was on to the next stop in his magical mystery victory tour, a campaign rally in Dalton, Georgia, on the eve of the Georgia special election.

It was a long painful speech, a Greatest Hits album of Trumpisms. Interspersed with faint praise for Republican candidates David Perdue and Kelly Loeffler were long stretches of specious facts, bald-faced lies and "numbers" from his experts showing how it was impossible for him to lose this election.

For Trump, it's all about the numbers. Maybe that's a holdover from his real estate days. In his mind, he got 12 million more votes in 2020 than in 2016. In any other year, that would have won him a Pollie as Campaign Manager of the Year. But Joe Biden got 15 million more votes than Hillary Clinton did in 2016. Sleepy Joe? Trump couldn't wrap his head around that.

On stage, Trump was like an old prizefighter bobbing, jabbing, throwing every punch in his repertoire.

"We will not bend, we will not yield, we will never give in, we will never give up, we will never back down, we will never, ever surrender, because we are America, and we are from Georgia, and our hearts bleed red, white and blue," he said.

An Umbrella of Fraud

I've been scratching my head for weeks trying to figure out what makes Trump loyalists think they have to step in to overturn a presidential election. The president has unburdened all his grievances on Twitter under the umbrella of vote fraud. But no matter how often he posts—even in all caps—saying it doesn't make it so.

His legal team has botched its case in every courtroom they appeared. His devotees on Fox News—the Sean Hannitys, Tucker Carlsons and Lou Dobbs of the world—fill the airwaves with so-called evidence that is as thin as a rumor. Fox then bundles these allegations together into a Chyron ribbon—"Massive Voter Fraud"—that lingers on screen from daypart to daypart as if it were an accepted fact.

This week, one Trump Republican after another has gone on Fox to announce they feel compelled to challenge the Electoral College because their constituents are concerned about massive voter fraud, but those concerns are based on what they are seeing on Fox. So Trump and Fox have created this endless loop of disinformation that leaves no room for one critical detail. Trump lost the election. Big time.

A Conspiracy, Not a Fraud

When proof of election fraud failed to materialize, Trump loyalists turned to a new theory of the case propounded by Mark Levin, a rising star on the right. Levin has a radio show carried on 300 stations and a Sunday night talk show on Fox. He appears frequently on Hannity as a legal expert and delivers his opinions like they are written on stone tablets handed down by God.

Levin's contention is that Democrats, in their drive to encourage more voter participation, bypassed state legislatures in battleground states to "systematically and strategically" shift the ground under election procedures.

"The Democrat Party, its surrogates, and eventually the Biden campaign instituted an unprecedented legal and lobbying campaign, mostly under the radar, to undermine our Constitution, the Republican state legislatures, and the Trump reelection campaign, in favor of Biden." In other words, they tried to win.

So President Trump really wasn't the victim of vote fraud, he was the victim of a conspiracy. The Democrats didn't so much break the election rules as change them. They registered more Democrats than Republicans. They promoted mail-in voting (Trump did not) to overcome voter fears of going to the polls during the coronavirus pandemic. In Milwaukee, they put ballot drop boxes in inner-city neighborhoods for senior citizens who had difficulty getting to the polls. In Georgia, they reversed Republican efforts in past elections to limit polling sites and restrict hours in Black neighborhoods. In Pennsylvania, they won a court order allowing ballots postmarked by Election Day to be counted up to three days later.

Outwitted and Outplayed

In the words of Trump's favorite producer Mark Burnett, the Democrats outwitted, outplayed and outlasted the Republicans. Now Trump wants a do-over because he couldn't find the Immunity Idol?

There's no way to pin a 7 million vote discrepancy on a lost ballot box here, or a faulty machine there, or not enough poll watchers in Philadelphia. The votes that beat Trump were everywhere, a lot of them from people who nobody ever thought to ask before.

After four tumultuous years with President Trump, Republicans and Democrats were eager to step forward and voice their opinion last November, and doing it was easier than ever. Trump's numbers were up. Biden's numbers were up. You really want to know why Trump lost? Because turnout in 2020 was 66.3%, versus 60% in 2016, in a country that is growing more diverse every day. And enough of them were so fed up with the president they got together and voted him out of office.

"If this outcome is allowed to stand without a fight, it will become extremely difficult for Republicans to win nationwide elections (something the 10 or so GOP senators who wish to run for president should keep in mind)," Levin said, getting to the crux of the issue. "The Democrat Party's goal is to turn the nation's electoral system into one-party rule. They are playing for keeps and destroying our constitutional system, for which they have little regard. [Republicans] must make it clear to the Democrats that we, the people, who believe in this Republic, will not roll over!"

We're Not Going to Take It Anymore

Congress convened to count the Electoral College votes under a bleak, chilly sky. A mile away on the Ellipse across from the White House, Trump was addressing a "Save America" rally. His speech was a 75-minute brain dump of all the nonsense swirling around in his head. ("Trump is speaking now. He is lying about the election. It's not worth tweeting," reported Daniel Dale, the CNN fact checker.)

"We're not going to take it anymore," Trump shouted. "We're going to walk down Pennsylvania Avenue—I love Pennsylvania Avenue—and we're going to the Capitol, and we're going to try and give our Republicans, the weak ones because the strong ones don't need any of our help, we're going to try to give them the kind of pride and boldness they need to take back our country."

Mo Brooks, the Alabama congressman, picked up where Trump left off. "Today is a day for choosing, and tomorrow is a day for fighting," he said. "Today is the day America's patriots start taking names and kicking ass. Are you willing to do what it takes to fight for America?"

"Fight for Trump," the crowd roared.

Then Brooks quoted from Revolutionary War hero Tom Paine. "The summer soldier and the sunshine patriot will, in this crisis, shrink from the service of their country; but he that stands by it now, deserves the love and thanks of man and woman. Tyranny, like hell, is not easily conquered; yet we have this consolation with us, that the harder the conflict, the more glorious the triumph."

May You Live in Interesting Times

As Brooks' speech wound down, thousands of MAGA heads were streaming down Pennsylvania Avenue toward the Capitol. They clashed with police, broke down a succession of protective barriers and stormed the Capitol steps. Scores of them made it inside, breaking windows, vandalizing offices and halting sessions in both the House and Senate. They roamed the halls, posed for selfies in the Rotunda, hung a Trump flag on the balcony, and occupied the Senate floor. Capitol police stood with guns drawn in the House chamber to keep them at bay. Legislators were forced to hide in undisclosed locations. The mahogany cases that held the Electoral College votes were whisked away to a safe location.

President Trump, meanwhile, left the rally and immediately went back to the White House where he continued to tweet about Mike Pence betraying him by following the Constitution. For two hours, he said nothing about the violence in the Capitol.

Back to Normal

After six hours of chaos, order was restored to the Capitol and Congress resumed debate on a routine motion leading to a foregone conclusion. At 3:40 a.m., Vice President Pence announced that Congress accepts the fact Joseph R. Biden Jr. will be the next president of the United States by a vote of 92 to 8 in the Senate, and 282 to 138 in the House.

And President Trump tweeted.

"These are the things and events that happen when a sacred landslide election victory is so unceremoniously & viciously stripped away from great patriots who have been badly & unfairly treated for so long. Go home with love & in peace. Remember this day forever!"

— January 7, 2021

Impeachment, Again

IF YOU WATCHED THE NEWS FRIDAY NIGHT, you went to sleep wondering what the story of the day was. Was it the House of Representatives pushing ahead with impeachment? Or Twitter yanking Donald Trump's account? Or maybe, the United States setting a new record of 4,112 COVID-19 deaths in a single day.

The news was punishing on all fronts, because the President-Who-Won't-Go-Away has made sure his last 10 days in office will overshadow Joe Biden's first.

Did Trump mean it when he read that video condemning the violence in the Capitol? Will Congress impeach him? Will he call for more protests? What other crazy stunt will he pull?

These are perilous times, passions are inflamed, and the country is in dire need of solutions to a raging pandemic, so let me suggest a way forward. Chill out.

Impeachment #2

Democrats in the House are lined up behind articles of impeachment that charge President Trump "gravely endangered the security of the United States...threatened the integrity of the democratic system, interfered with the peaceful transition of power, and imperiled a coordinate branch of government."

House Speaker Nancy Pelosi says the impeachment resolution could pass as early as Monday. As we learned last time around in Impeachment #1, House leaders will then ceremoniously walk the petition over to the Senate for trial. But nobody is better at slow walking than Senate Majority Leader Mitch McConnell, who says the Senate will not be back in session to receive it until Jan. 19, Trump's last day in office.

Since we are harking back in history, remember the first trial for Impeachment #1 took 16 days. Setting aside the constitutional issue of whether a president can be impeached after he leaves office—and don't do it too quickly because we know how litigious Trump is—that means the Senate will spend the first weeks of the Biden administration listening to lawyers debate whether the assault on the Capitol was an "insurrection" (Anderson Cooper) or "a political protest that got out of hand" (Tucker Carlson). Did the president start the fire or just fan the flames?

And while we're not on the topic, let's use the Senate trial to rehash the evidence that the Democrats stole the election.

This impeachment effort will fail, just as the first one did, for lack of the 67 Senate votes needed to convict. Meanwhile, it will extend the grip Trump has on the nation's psyche—exacerbating the current political divide—and give him an opportunity to claim the lack of a conviction means I'M INNOCENT. Assume all the Democrats in the new 50-50 party split in the Senate will go for it. Add in Republicans who've already declared Trump unfit. Mitt Romney, Ben Sasse, Lisa Murkowski, Pat Toomey and Susan Collins. Where are the other 12 Republican senators going to come from?

'Unhinged'

Pelosi is right to be concerned about the president's mental health (although his behavior is not all that different than it's been for four years). Her preferred way of dealing with Trump's lunacy would be the 25th Amendment, but there are not enough rational people left in the cabinet to invoke it. "He's unhinged," she's been telling Democratic friends. "We aren't talking about anything besides an unhinged person."

She's not the first to notice. Omarosa Manigault's book about her years in the White House was also called *Unhinged*. The likelihood Trump will do something stupid has always been there, but the guardrails are down this time, and the president appears to be hunkered down with a little coterie of loyalists in the White House, still thinking he won the election.

Phil Rucker, Ashley Parker and Josh Dawsey have covered all four years of the Trump White House for *The Washington Post*. After the attack on the Capitol, they wrote this account of what it was like that night:

"President Trump spent more than 24 hours after instigating a mob to violently storm the Capitol trying to escape reality. Cloistered in the White House, Trump raged uncontrollably about perceived acts of betrayal. He tuned out advisers who pleaded with him to act responsibly. He was uninterested in trying to repair what he had wrought. And he continued to insist he won the election, even as his own vice president certified the fact he had not."

The *Post* describes Trump's mood as indignant, unmoored and psychologically fragile. In the afternoon, Trump watched the attack on the Capitol play out on television "bemused" by the spectacle of his supporters literally fighting for him. He didn't like the costumes on the people rummaging through the Capitol. He thought they looked "low class," but he made no attempt to call off his legions.

He was so mad at Pence "he couldn't see straight." He walked around berating his most loyal follower, and he never called the Capitol to ask if Pence was all right. "I made this guy, I saved him from a political death, and here he stabs me in the back," Trump bellowed.

"Only after darkness fell in Washington on Thursday, after the Capitol had been besieged by death and destruction and a growing chorus of lawmakers had called for his immediate removal from office, did Trump grudgingly accept his fate," the *Post* reported.

He agreed to make a short video accepting the fact "a new administration" would be inaugurated Jan. 20 and calling for "healing and reconciliation." But he couldn't get through it without throwing in an aside on vote fraud. He never used the word "concede."

He regretted doing it almost as soon as it was over. Then in the midst of it all, Twitter announced it was suspending his account. They were taking away his toys.

"He is alone. He is mad King George," a Trump confidant told the *Post*.

The New Enemy of the People

Impeachment will only sate Trump's craving to get back in the limelight. Better to let him stew in his own juices. Over the weekend, the FBI arrested dozens of Capitol crazies. Let the Justice Department go after the perpetrators one at a time. Hanging over every trial, or in defendant's plea, will be the words, "I did it because the president told me to." Torture Trump with the slow drip of the consequences that came from his words.

And what will Trump do next? The best thing that happened Thursday night was Twitter shut him down. They took away his voice. They violated his right to free speech. And that made him mad.

Twitter was his signature form of expression: Think it, say it. Don't worry if it's right—or spelled correctly. This was his only way of talking to his followers without the media getting in the way. He tried to tweet an FU back on his official @Potus account. Twitter shut it down. He posted a screed on @Team Trump about "Democrats and the Radical Left removing my account to silence me—and YOU, the 75,000,000 great patriots who voted for me." Twitter shut that down.

An alarmed Don Jr. tweeted a warning to followers of his account. "Guys, assuming the purge of conservative ideas and thought leaders continues here and on other social platforms take 2 seconds and shoot me your email. That way if/when they cancel me, I can let you all know where I land."

"If he really wants to be heard, he can walk his lazy ass to the briefing room and start yapping," Jon Favreau, President Obama's former speechwriter and host of *Pod Save America*, tweeted. Eventually, that's what the president did, not in person, but by issuing a statement on White House letterhead announcing he was searching for alternative social networks and promising to build a new internet platform that will be the greatest thing since Space Force. Great idea, Mr. President. You get right on that.

By the end of the week, Trump was banned on Twitter, Facebook, Instagram, Snapchat, YouTube, Reddit, Twitch, and TikTok due to the risk he might incite more violence.

But now Trump has a new target for his wrath. A new windmill to tilt at. Big Tech. This is a speech he's given before. Big Tech is trying to silence him, taking away our most basic freedoms, driving our politics to the Marxist, socialist left and, needless to say, ruining America.

Big Tech. Now there's an enemy worth his Big Wrath.

Change Is Coming

In one of those cable dayparts nobody watches, I saw Colin Powell, the former secretary of state, interviewed by Anderson Cooper. He didn't know whether impeachment would work. "I just want him to go. Put him on Air Force One and send him off golfing at Mar-a-Lago."

There are important changes that must come in America, and no time to waste not doing them. Let Trump be Trump, somewhere else. If you remember, we elected a new president in November. His name is Joe Biden, and here is what he had to say on the subject:

"If we were six months out, we should be moving everything to get him out of office, impeaching him again, trying to invoke the 25th Amendment, whatever it took to get him out of office. But I am focused now on us taking control as president and vice president on the 20th, and to get our agenda moving as quickly as we can."

Amen to that. There's a pandemic raging. Let's let the government get back into the business of governing.

— January 10, 2021

Unity

WELL, THE PROBLEMS STACKED UP PRETTY FAST for Donald Trump after he gave that Save America speech and incited a riot at the Capitol. His Twitter account was canceled, the PGA yanked its golf championship from Bedminster, Mitch McConnell stopped talking to him, Deutsche Bank said it won't do any new business with him, and House Republican leader Kevin McCarthy urged him to make a conciliatory call to Joe Biden to show "unity."

Not to mention, Nancy Pelosi has all her ducks lined up for an impeachment vote. Mike Pence, once as close to Trump as a leach, is missing in action. Probably off in his special place asking God whether to invoke the 25th Amendment. (At 10 p.m., Pence issued a statement. God said no.) And there are eight more days until Trump leaves office, one way or another. This is going to be great theater.

Breaking News

I've been watching all this unfold at home on the cable channels, lying on the couch trying not to get Covid. My favorite channel (*NewsMix*) gives me a quad-split of CNN, FOX, MSNBC and the BBC live so I can click around between them to get all sides. I stay away from the TV on most mornings, but at noon I try to catch Brianna Keilar's *Breaking News* to get the lay of the land.

In bullet-point fashion, she reported today:

- The House is buttoning up an impeachment resolution they will pass if the president doesn't resign.
- President Trump is off to Alamo, Texas, to inspect his wall. Lindsey Graham, his best and/or last friend, is going along as the designated driver.
- Mike Pompeo suddenly called off his visit to NATO allies. "Something you wouldn't do unless something was up," Brianna noted.
- The FBI sent out a bulletin warning of right-wing militias rallying in state capitals, seizing government buildings, surrounding the Capitol and otherwise disrupting the inauguration. "This is an organized group that has a plan," Rep. Conor Lamb told CNN. "We're talking about thousands of people, with published rules of engagement."
- And Fox has an exclusive clip of Trump on the runway to Texas saying his Save America Speech on Jan. 6 was "totally appropriate." Nancy Pelosi's move to impeach him, he added, "is really a continuation of the greatest witch hunt in the history of politics. It's ridiculous I think it will cause tremendous anger."

Mike Huckabee interpreted Trump's remarks for his Fox audience to mean "Impeachment shows tremendous disrespect—not only for Trump but for the 75 million people who voted for him. The Democrats are making a big mistake. This is a time for unity."

Treading Water

After Brianna's breaking news, the cable channels tread water in the early afternoon waiting to see whether anything she predicted comes true. That gave MSNBC a chance to check in at the White House with correspondent Shannon Pettypiece to see how it was going.

"The White House right now feels like a poorly run startup company. It is just chaos," she reported. "Plans are being made and canceled. No one has clear answers to things. Last week we were told the president was going to Camp David, then we were told he wasn't going. Yesterday, we were told there could be some remarks coming around 7. There were no remarks. Again today, there's some sort of hastily organized trip where the local authorities weren't notified. We have no idea what's on the president's schedule for the rest of the week.

"This is how things are ending in the Trump administration. This is what the last week looks like."

All Hat, No Cattle

The president's plane landed in Texas around 2 p.m. He stepped to a lectern and read from scripted remarks.

"Free speech is under assault like never before. Now is the time for our nation to heal…It's time for peace and calm…We've done a great job on the vaccines. You know it's tough to make a vaccine…They said it would take years and years, but we delivered it…They're calling it a medical miracle…"

Click. The only channel carrying Trump live was Fox, and they cut him off like a loose fingernail when they saw all the other cable channels were streaming live from the FBI press conference on the Capitol riot.

Trump was alone now, all hat and no cattle. The focus was no longer on him. The focus was on the wreckage he left in his wake.

Insurrection

I've been calling it a riot, but as the FBI made clear, it was a lot more than that. It was an assault on the Capitol building by right-wing militants, organized for the purpose of keeping Donald Trump in office. It was brutal, dangerous and coordinated over the internet on the right-wing chat channels.

Over 70 people have been arrested, and hundreds more are under investigation. The potential charges range from trespassing to murder to sedition. The FBI has over 100,000 video clips, tweets and posts to help identify the perpetrators. More are coming in every day.

The Ebb and Flow of News

By 5:30 p.m., the ebb and flow of stories in the cable news channels usually gets funneled down into four or five minutes on the network news. The headline package on NBC paired Mitch McConnell saying he thought the Capitol insurrection was "impeachable" with Republican House leader Liz Cheney announcing she would vote for impeachment. "The president of the United States summoned this mob, assembled the mob and lit the flame of this attack," she said. Impeachment was gaining steam. Within the hour, five more House Republicans signed on.

The roller coaster is back on track. We're going to hear a lot more about it in the next few days. But the one thing everybody agrees on. We need more unity.

— January 12, 2021

The Last Hurrah

THE RATINGS FOR THE HOUSE IMPEACHMENT DEBATE Wednesday must have really chafed Donald Trump's butt. Twelve million viewers. *Celebrity Apprentice* got more than that on a bad day. They're going to cancel his presidency next week, and no one is going to be watching.

I mean, he already gave the media wolves what they wanted. He said what his lawyers told him he had to say. They wrote it out for him in a scripted little video nobody watched. He abhors the violence and wants to heal the nation's wounds. Crap like that. If he still had his Twitter account, he could have done it better. But they're taking a lot of things away from him these days, just like they took away his reelection.

The president is walking around the White House in a forest of cardboard boxes. People are packing their things, saying goodbye, moving on. Kellyanne Conway is gone. Kayleigh McEnany. Mick Mulvaney. Hope Hicks bugged out. And Rudy Giuliani is still in the doghouse for all the postelection work he botched.

On the day of the House impeachment hearings, the president drifted in and out of the Oval Office, monitoring the proceedings on TV, according to *The Washington Post*. At one point, he told aides he wanted to go over there to give them a piece of his mind, but they said that's not how it works. And he doesn't have that many pieces left to give away.

Jim Acosta, the chief White House reporter for CNN, says the usual bustle of advisers is down to a handful. Mark Meadows, Dan Savino, his personal twitterer (who has a lot of time on his hands), senior policy adviser Stephen Miller and Robert O'Brien, his national security adviser. Lindsey Graham calls to check in, but other friends are deeply concerned about his state of mind. They think the president is "clueless" about how bad this looks, Acosta says. "He essentially has no clue how much this has damaged his standing in the history books, and how much this has damaged the standing of the United States on the world stage."

Trump could have spent his last days in office organizing the vaccine response, finding out the extent of the latest Russian cyberattack, preparing an impeachment defense, tamping down the latest threats from North Korea, or, God forbid, helping President-elect Biden get ready for the challenges ahead.

Instead, Acosta reports, he's consumed by worries about what all this is doing to his brand. "He is fearful that when he leaves office, his businesses are going to be in serious trouble because of all this. The president faces the real prospect of going broke after his accumulation of debts, because of the stain on the Trump brand, and so on."

Acosta gave his report on CNN moments after the House impeachment vote. He had just spoken with a senior White House adviser, who had just spoken with Trump. Costa read from notes to make sure he was quoting Trump's friend accurately:

"In the end, it all came crashing down because Donald Trump could never tell the truth. He will be the cautionary tale that parents tell their kids. Don't end up like Trump because of your lies."

"I think that's an extraordinary statement," Acosta said. "Even his own people know he's a scoundrel. They know he's a liar. They know he's somebody that incites violence because he can't admit that he lost the 2020 election. It was a lie that became so cancerous it brought on his downfall."

A Patriot Jamboree

Word is Trump wants a big send-off when he leaves the White House. A last hurrah. We just don't know what it will be, or when it will happen. Maybe this weekend. FBI reports say as many as 100,000 armed protesters have been called to Washington for a "Save the Second Amendment Rally."

That, at least, is what how it was described on the dark web before the post was taken down. Now, they are rallying for free speech, so let's call them armed free-speech advocates.

National Guard troops are sleeping in the Capitol waiting for them. Protective measures are being taken to safeguard D.C. bridges and government buildings. The National Mall will be closed. Airbnb has canceled all reservations. The TSA will be screening all incoming flights to root out suspicious passengers. All eyes will be on Washington to see if America is capable of functioning as a free and democratic nation.

What are the chances Donald Trump won't try to put himself in the middle of it? If he wants to come across as the champion of America, he can hold that military parade he always wanted, marching the National Guard down Pennsylvania like it's the Champs-Elysees, in dress camo with surveillance drones flying in formation overhead.

He can give a speech, a peaceful speech, a beautiful speech, thanking all the patriots who stood by him through these difficult times. The Beach Boys will sing. He'll gather his family on stage behind him to wave goodbye, and a helicopter will whisk them off to Mar-a-Lago with a military band playing "Hail to the Chief."

Except, he won't leave. The helicopter will circle back to the White House for one last gathering of MAGA nation. He'll give out free vaccines.

No one will have to wear masks. People can talk about all the money they made before the plague set in. They'll light a bonfire on the South Lawn and have fireworks over the Washington Monument. If you hear the sound of AR-15 gunfire in the air, well that's just Proud Boys being Proud Boys. Everything will be just as he imagined it would be—if he won.

— January 15, 2021

The Mob
Was Fed Lies

OF THE 30,000 LIES DONALD TRUMP HAS TOLD in his presidency, the one Mitch McConnell will never forget is the one that almost got him killed.

In the well of the Senate, on the day before the inauguration of Joe Biden, McConnell remembered the events on Jan. 6 like they were yesterday. "The last time the Senate convened, we had just reclaimed the Capitol from violent criminals who tried to stop Congress from doing our duty," he began.

Just thinking about it made McConnell shudder. He was in the Senate chamber when the Capitol insurrection started. Finally, Donald Trump had run out his string of loser excuses and Congress was ready to affirm the Electoral College votes. The envelopes from each state would be opened, Congress would count the votes, and Vice President Pence would make the ceremonial proclamation.

McConnell had given Trump all the rope he needed to make his case that the election was stolen, but in courtroom after courtroom he presented no evidence. His options were down to slim and none. McConnell knew it was time to move on. But the president was so obsessed by the idea he'd really won, McConnell stopped talking to him a month ago.

Now that they were down to open the box, count the votes and raise your right hand, McConnell could see the process going off the rails. The president had hyped up all the Trumpkins on his side of the aisle to "object" to the Electoral College tally, and to make matters worse, he was out on the Mall egging his MAGA Army on. "We fight. We fight like Hell and if you don't fight like Hell, you're not going to have a country anymore."

While the president was speaking, McConnell explained to his fellow Senators why he would NOT object to the Electoral College decision. "We're debating a step that has never been taken in American history. Whether Congress should overrule the voters and overturn a presidential election…. The voters, the courts, and the states have all spoken. If we overrule them it would damage our Republic forever…I will vote to respect the people's decision and defend our system of government as we know it."

McConnell called it the most important vote he has cast in his 36 years in Congress. Forty minutes after he finished, the first rioters broke down the doors of the Capitol.

In the Well

Two weeks after the Capitol insurrection, with National Guardsmen stationed in the Capitol corridors, McConnell was back in the well to assure the incoming president he would help him make a smooth transition.

But he could still hear the echo of the mob raging through the hallway. "Hang Mike Pence!" they shouted. "Where's Nancy's office?" He remembered the savage look on the face of the rioters, hearing a gunshot in the distance, the Secret Service whisking away the vice president, getting pulled down the hall into a secret room with Chuck Schumer, Nancy Pelosi and Kevin McCarthy.

"The mob was fed lies," he said. "They were provoked by the president and other powerful people." He spoke slowly. Deliberately, now speaking for the whole institution. "We stood together and said an angry mob would not have veto power over the rule of law in our nation, not even for one night. We certified the people's choice for their 46th president."

A Man of Decorum

Mitch McConnell is no spring chicken. He's 78 (and was just reelected for six more years). He's been the leader of Senate Republicans—sometimes in the majority, sometimes not—for 15 years. He appreciates Thomas Jefferson's description of the Senate as the saucer that cools the hot tea of the House, and he has wielded that saucer with all the decorum of Cicero in the Forum, because McConnell loves decorum.

But decorum was the last thing from his mind in that secret room with Chuck and Nancy and Kevin. The room was not soundproof. He could hear the caterwauling outside, the thugs with their ropes, and ladders, and handcuffs, the sound of windows being smashed and pepper gas grenades.

All the leaders had cellphones, so they were getting firsthand reports from aides or instant videos showing the chaos in the corridors. McConnell saw rioters rummaging through the desks of senators, a clown in coonskin hat and bullhorns preening on the Senate dais. They were attacking the Senate. Invading the Senate. Defiling the Senate. His Senate! It scared the shit out of him.

Locked away together, the congressional leaders reached out to their contacts at the Pentagon to find out when the National Guard was coming. (An aide to the secretary of the Army told them it was being held back because of the "optics.") Finally, the Pentagon released the guard, but it took two hours for the troops to arrive. Two hours locked in a room with Nancy Pelosi, Mitch McConnell, Chuck Schumer and Kevin McCarthy in the middle of a riot. What would you do? I'd shoot myself.

But Mitch McConnell came away with a different perspective. Democracy was under attack, and if it survived, he was going to do more to preserve it. The Senate would do things different in the next couple years. They'd work together. Trust in the government would not be restored until the people saw it working.

"Certainly November's elections did not hand any side a mandate for sweeping ideological change," McConnell said. "Our marching orders from the American people are clear: We're to have a robust discussion and seek common ground…We are to pursue bipartisan agreement everywhere we can…and check and balance one another respectfully where we must."

As McConnell spoke, he knew an impeachment resolution was coming his way. Trump's remarks outside the Capitol had, indeed, provoked the crowd, and that was an impeachable offense. When the resolution came before the Senate, he was going to tell senators to vote their conscience. He hadn't made up his mind how he would vote—he needed to take the temperature of the saucer—but he had made up his conscience.

Meanwhile, Back at the Ranch

After McConnell's speech wound down, MSNBC switched its cameras over to the White House. The usually busy front portico steps were empty. No cabinet members were going in or out. The president had not been seen all day.

Sources said he was working on his farewell address, a five-minute video he'd been practicing, so it was coming in around 20. The Associated Press reporter gave it a brutal review. "He claimed credit for things he didn't do and twisted his record on jobs, taxes, the pandemic and much more," he wrote. "Falsehoods suffused his farewell remarks to the country."

It was a speech written for a time capsule. The words on the teleprompter had been worked over more times than a Kayleigh McEnany fact. But without an audience, the president's delivery was flat.

In a future Trump presidential library, the Trump hologram on a pedestal in the rotunda will probably will not be giving his Farewell Address: words he didn't write, delivered to no one, in an empty White House. Or maybe it will. What else are you going to put there? Stormy Daniels?

The Sound of Silence

Across the Mall at the Lincoln Memorial, Joe Biden and Kamala were attending a memorial service for the 400,000 Americas who have died from COVID-19. Orange lamps lined the sides of the Reflecting Pool converging on the Washington Monument. When the ceremony ended, they turned and stood quietly looking out at the breathless beauty of it all.

You could feel the silence. It was a blessed silence. The Trump years were over.

Inauguration Day

Inauguration Day ran like clockwork.

President Trump refused to attend Biden's swearing in ceremony, the first sitting president not to attend since Andrew Johnson. Instead, he invited anyone who worked at the White House, or ever had worked at the White House (and wasn't busy getting ready for the inauguration) to come to Andrews Air Force Base to see him off. There was a red carpet, a military band playing "Hail to the Chief" and maybe a couple hundred people, mostly friends and family. As he walked to Air Force One, Trump's last words were, "We will be back in some form. Have a good life."

Exactly three minutes after Air Force One went wheels up, Joe and Jill Biden emerged from St. Matthews Cathedral, the traditional first stop at the inauguration of an incoming president. They then went to Arlington National Cemetery, attended a reception in the Capitol and embarked on all the rituals of the day. The swearing in, the poem, the song, the speech, the handshaking, and the inexhaustible blather on TV about what an historic occasion this is.

Notes and Clippings

With the TV on in the background, I started sifting through my notes and clippings to find things I meant to use but couldn't find a place for. They were a jumble of random observations, kind of like a Trump speech, and it occurred to me the best way to end this story might be to put this jumble together into a conclusion.

Here, for instance, is Tom Friedman writing in *The New York Times* after the election. "We have just experienced four years of the most divisive and dishonest presidency in American history, which attacked the twin pillars of our democracy—truth and trust. Donald Trump has not spent a single day of his term trying to be president of all the people, and he has broken rules and trashed norms in ways that no other president ever dared."

And here's Rich Lowry, editor of the *National Review*: "Trump is, for better or worse, the foremost symbol of resistance to the overwhelming woke cultural tide that has swept along the media, academia, corporate America, Hollywood, professional sports, the big foundations, and almost everything in between," Lowry wrote. "To put it in blunt terms, he's the only middle finger available—to brandish against the people who've assumed they have the whip hand in American culture."

On *CBS This Morning*, Anthony Mason observed, "To meet Donald Trump for the first time is to meet him forever. He is exactly the same in everything he does, and it's all about him."

I have snippets of commentary from the right-wing echo chamber. Sean Hannity bloviating on this and that. Rush Limbaugh making Trump's reelection his dying wish. Lou Dobbs saying he can't believe Trump lost. How could the greatest president in the history of the United States lose? And Rudy Giuliani touting lawsuits that never came to fruition.

On his last day in office, Trump was still bobbing and weaving to avoid saying Joe Biden won the election. Nicolle Wallace looked like she wanted to spank him as she watched his farewell video. "All he has to say is one sentence. He has to say, 'I lost fair and square.' All this was a lie. I really, really liked playing president. But I lost. That's it.'"

The Anchor

There are a few journalists in every generation who anchor the nightly news desks and, in just the right tone and timber, with an instinct for saying the right thing at the right moment, reflect the mood of the nation. Brian Williams has done that for me throughout this weird journey, but especially on the day the House voted to impeach Trump for a second time.

"This president will now leave office having lost the House, Senate and White House. Having lost reelection. Having lost the popular vote twice," he said. "As of today, and as children will be taught in schools for the rest of our days, Donald John Trump of Queens, New York, becomes the first president in our history to be impeached twice.

"The man who warned us we would get tired of winning has now lost everything. His place in history has now been cemented. The man we heard on tape trying to rig the outcome of an election he lost. The man whose malfeasance, malpractice and enablers will forever be linked with an American death toll now approaching 400,000 souls. Trump will now be tried as an ex-president, a real gut check of the gutless, the ultimate test of the Republicans who sold out their names and offices to become the party of Donald Trump."

The End

Mitch McConnell will never forget the lie that almost brought down our democracy. The web of conspiratorial theories Trump wove about election fraud were just his way of covering up the fact he ran a half-assed campaign for an office he was ill-equipped to hold.

The lies he told matter. The false notion his election was stolen will be ingrained forever in American history. But the lies are just one way of keeping score.

Donald Trump has pretty much golfed his way through his presidency. He has a lot of clubs in his bag, and he's been taking divots out of the American character all across the country. He's mean, stupid, selfish, insensitive, uninformed, and unfit to be president. And in the end, all those failings rose to the surface.

It's like I told you. He's an asshole.

Epilogue

The Note in the Desk

When a new president comes into office, it's traditional for the outgoing president to leave him a note in the Resolute Desk. Barack Obama's read, "We are just temporary occupants of this office. It's up to us to leave the instruments of this democracy at least as strong as we found them."

President Trump's was a little less formal.

Sleepy Joe—

You don't deserve this, but Ivanka says I have to write one of these for my legacy. So here are a few tips.

—Garbage pickup is Wednesdays. They take the recyclables on Thursday, but we don't do that. It's just another Save The Planet Hoax. TOTAL WASTE OF TIME.

—Melania's Christmas decorations are in the basement. You know, the ones that made it look like we're the Addams Family. You can toss them. I never liked them anyway.

—The *Webster Guide to Misspelling* is in the upper left desk drawer. Now that they took away my Twitter, I don't need it. BUT I'M TAKING ALL THE CAPITAL LETTERS.

—I rewired the Kremlin hotline to go straight to the pro shop at Bedford. I don't need it. I have Putin's cell. If you ever want a tee time, they can fit you in. So have a round on me. Remember. Rake the traps!

—Mike Pence used to like to come in sometimes and sit in the foyer in case I needed him. That's why he's in so many pictures. He'll be back. He has nothing else to do.

—And speaking of no-accounts. Don't fix up the press room. Those guys treat it like it's their own little clubhouse. AND THEY'RE SLOBS! The hand sanitizer is on the left when you go in.

—Good luck. You'll need it. The country is a mess.

Donald Trump

Photo Credits

7 Republicans Day One, photo by Joe Raedle, Getty images

9 Lock Her Up, photo by Pete Marovich/ UPI/Alamy Stock Photo

15 Pence on Fire, photo by Mark Reinstein/Shutterstock

19 Our Mussolini, photo by Mike Segar/ Reuters /stock.adobe.com

27 Heavy Lift, photo by Mark Kauzlarich/Reuters/Alamy Stock Photo

31 Punch In the Mouth!, Hoo Me/Storms Media Group/Alamy Stock Photo

35 The Has-Been, photo by Susan Walsh/AP Images

39 One Man's Opinion photo by Rick Wilking/Reuters/ stock.adobe.com

47 Can We Talk, photo by Brennan Linsley/AP Images

63 Down the Rabbit Hole, illustration by James Steidl/ stock.adobe.com

75 All in on The Wall, photo by Samantha Sals/Reuters/ stock.adobe.com

79 Salesman in Chief, photo by Evan El-Amin/Shutterstock

85 The Environment Is Overrated, photo by Gary Miller courtesy of the National Archives

95 The First 100 days, photo courtesy of Columbia Pictures

103 The National Conversation, TV news analysis courtesy of The Shorenstein Center

104 The National Conversation, cable ratings courtesy of TV Newser

109 I am a Rock, photo courtesy of NATO via Blikk

115 Not the Only Show in Town, illustration courtesy of Scott Scheidly

119 The Lonely Life of I Alone, photo by Feliipe Trueba/EPA

125 Flying Bag of Dope, architectural rendering by the PennaGroup

137 The Russian Connection, photo from Extra TV

143   The Room Where It Happened, photo by Olivier Douliery/Abaca Press/Alamy Stock Photo

175   Keeping Score, photo by Kevin Lamarque/Reuters/ stock.adobe.com

177   To Mask or Not to Mask, photo courtesy of Neuroscience News

181   The Press Conference, photo by Jonathan Ernst/Reuters/ stock.adobe.com

185   Shoe on the Other Foot, photo by Jonathan Ernst/Reuters/ stock.adobe.com

191   Never in Doubt, photo by Spencer Platt/Getty Images

201   See You in Court, photo by John Minchillo/AP Images

215   LOSER, photo by Kevin Lamarque/Reuters/stock.adobe.com

225   'Tis the Season, photo by Lucas Jackson, Reuters/ stock.adobe.com

231   Avalanche of Corruption, meme via Liberals Are Cool

241   Constitutional Crisis, photo by Andrew Harnik/AP Images

249   Impeachment, Again, photo by Leah Mills/Reuters/ stock.adobe.com

255   Unity, photo by Photo by Shay Horse/NurPhoto/Getty Images

259   The Last Hurrah, meme via Jay@Bluewavesaveus

263   The Mob Was Fed Lies, photo by Shannon Staples/Reuters/ stock.adobe.com

Index

8kun 210

Acosta, Jim *CNN* 184, 195, 260–261

Agalarov, Aras 138, 140

Baio, Scott 8

Baker, Peter *New York Times* 181–182

Bannon, Steve 66–67

Barr, Atty Gen William, 152, 199, 205, 207

Bash, Dana *CNN* 105, 197

Biden, Joe
    2016 convention 31–33
    2020 election 191–199, 219, 220
    Inauguration 267

Biden, Hunter 151–152, 182

Blunt, Sen. Roy 187

Bolton, John
    In the Room Where It Happened 143–154
    Syria 145–146
    North Korea 146–148
    NATO meeting 148–150
    Putin Summit 150–151
    Ukraine 151–153

Booker, Sen. Cory 29

Border Wall, 75–78, 125–127, 234–235

Borger, Gloria *CNN* 11, 57, 105

Brooks, David 8, 101

Brooks, Rep. Mo 247–248

Bump, Philip *Washington Post* 127

Cable News Ratings 104

Capitol Insurrection 241–248, 257–258, 265–266

Carroll, E. Jean 207–208

Carson, Ben 12

Christie, Chris 11, 65

Cillizza, Chris *CNN* 113

Clinton, Bill 35–38

Clinton, Hillary

    2016 convention 39–43

    emails 55–56, 108

    husband Bill 35–38

    2016 election 50, 53–58

CNN 47, 57, 105–106, 193–194

Coal Country 92–93

Coats, Dan 150–151

Coney Barrett, Justice Amy 185–187

Conway, Kellyanne 80, 95, 223

Cooper, Anderson *CNN* 13, 105, 106, 198, 250

Cornyn, Sen John 186

COVID-19 176, 177–179, 219, 221–223, 231, 249

Cruz, Sen. Ted 16–17, 186, 199

Dale, Daniel *CNN* 183, 247

Debates, 56

Democratic Convention 27–43

Dionne, E.J. 101

Dobbs, Lou Fox 211–212, 268

Dominion Voting Systems 209–214

Dow Jones Average, 64, 233

Dowd, Maureen 112–113

Electoral College 191, 193, 199, 206, 215, 216, 232, 242,248, 264

Environmental Protection Agency (EPA) 85–93

Epshteyn, Boris 81

Ernst, Sen. Joni 187

Esformes, Philip 228–229

Favreau, Jon 253

Flynn, Michael 8, 11, 65, 131–136

Friedman, Thomas *New York Times* 268

Garamendi, Rep. John 232

Gardner, Sen. Cory 186

Gateway Pundit (Joe Hoft) 211–212

Graham, Sen. Lindsey 186, 198, 256, 260

Grassley, Sen. Chuck 186

Gruders, Joe 2

Grunwald, Michael *Politico* 97, 99

Hannity, Sean *FOX NEWS* 48, 108, 198, 210

Hoeven, Sen. John 187

Holt, Lester 197

Huckabee, Mike 17, 256

Immigration 234–235

Impeachment 69–73, 249–254

Inauguration Day 267

Johnson, Sen. Ron 186

Kaine, Sen. Tim 28

Karl, Jon *ABC* 195

Kasich, Gov. John 7

Keilar, Brianna *CNN* 256

Kelly, Gen. John 144, 146, 150

Kim Jong Un 98, 144, 146–148

King, John *CNN* 105, *magic wall* 193–194

Kinzinger, Rep. Adam 232, 244

Levin, Mark 246, 247

Limbaugh, Rush 102, 268

Lord, Jeffrey 57, 106

Lowry, Rich *National Review* 268

Macron, Emanuel 110, 112, 149

Maddow, Rachel *MSNBC* 57, 107

Mail-in voting 182, 191–199, 202, 206

Mason, Anthony *CBS* 268

Manafort, Paul 7, 16, 225–228

Manigault, Omarosa 251

Matthews, Chris *MSNBC* 107

Mattis, Gen. James 65, 98, 149, 244

McCain, Sen. John *health care* 122–123

McConnell, Mitch 11, 186–187, 255 *Capitol Insurrection* 263–266

McDaniel, Ronna RNC chair 210

McEnany, Kayleigh 57, 223, 229

McMaster, Gen. H.R. 144, 145

The Media 101–108

Merkel, Angela 111, 115, 149

Miller, Stephen 81, 260

Mohammed bin Salman 109

MSNBC 57, 106–107

Mueller Investigation 141, 150, 227–228

Mulvaney, Mick 90

NAFTA 98

NATO 110–111, 148–150, 256, *Der Spiegel* 112

New York Post 232

North Korea 98–99, 144, 146–147

Obama, Barack 64, 80, 86–87

Obama, Michelle 30

Obamacare 67–68

O'Donnell, Lawrence *MSNBC* 107

Our Bodies, Ourselves 42

Palin, Sarah 9

Parker, Ashley *Washington Post* 217, 251–252, 260

Pelosi, Speaker Nancy 250, 251 *Capitol Insurrection* 265

Pence, Mike 15, 17–18, 65, 134, 153, 182, 222, 242, 248, 252, 264, 273

Perdue, Sen. David 187, 204

Pettypiece, Shannon *MSNBC* 257

Pew Research Center 49, 51, 63, 116

Pompeo, Mike 146–147, 151, 256

Polls 28, 48, 183

Powell, Colin 253

Presidential Pardons 225–229

Priebus, Reince 56, 134

Putin, Vladimir, 132–134, 136, 138–139, 141, 150–151

Raffensperger, Brad 205, 242–244

Republican Convention 7–22

Rhuzkan, Ali F. 76–77

Rion, Chanel *OAN* 184, 212

Romney, Mitt 3, 251

Rubio, Sen. Marco 186

Rucker, *Phil Washington Post* 251–252, 260

Russia 131– 136, 137–142

Ryan, Paul 11, 67–68, 116, 233–234, 244

Sanders, Sen. Bernie 29

Sanders, Sarah 81, 120

Sasse, Sen. Ben 13, 251

Sater, Felix 139

Schieffer, Bob *CBS* 11

Scott, Sen. Rick 16

Sekulow, Jay 151, 210

Shorenstein Center 103–104

Simon, Roger *Politico* 10

Smerconish, Michael *CNN* 11

Snail Darter, rare and endangered 89

Spicer, Sean 9, 17, 80, 83, 96, 104, 111, 120, 134, 136

Stephanopoulos, George *ABC* 81

Stephens, Bret *Wall Street Journal* 49

Stone, Roger 134, 138, 226–228

Sykes, Charlie 49, 113, 182

Tapper, Jake *CNN* 29, 105, 195, 197

Todd, Chuck 18

Trump, Donald
  2016 convention
    introduces Melania 8
    I Alone Speech, 19–22
    Hillary Clinton, 21–22
    2016 election 53–58
    2020 election 191–199
    golf courses 91–92
    health care 79–83
    Wharton degree 159
    America First 113, 235
    The Apprentice 43, 66, 82–83, 259
    Twitter 56, 81, 98, 103, 115–117, 120, 133, 144, 155, 192–193, 203, 207, 211, 216, 245, 249, 252–253, 273
Trump, Melania 8, 9, 15–16, 223, 273
Trump, Donald Jr, 10, 12, 138, 140, 141, 151, 253
Trump, Eric 16, 134, 135
Trump Territory (Freeport, IL) 49–51
Trump Tower Meeting 140–142
Twitter 155–170
Unemployment 57, 175–176, 232
Vichy Republicans 203
Wallace, Nicolle *MSNBC* 57, 105, 106, 198, 268
Wasserman Schultz, Debbie 29, 56
Watergate 101
Wikileaks 29, 139, 227
Williams, Brian *MSNBC* 18, 107, 268–269
Will, George 183–184
Zelensky, Volodymyr 151–153
Zervos, Summer 208
Zorn, Eric *Chicago Tribune* 126
Zurawik, David *Baltimore Sun* 104